first 15

© First15

No part of this publication may be reproduced, distributed or transmitted in any form or by any means, including photocopying or electronic or mechanical method without prior written permission of the editor; except in the case of brief quotations embodied in critical reviews and certain other noncommercial uses permitted by copyright law. For permissions request, please write to us.

"Scripture quotations are from The ESV® Bible (The Holy Bible, English Standard Version®), copyright © 2001 by Crossway, a publishing ministry of Good News Publishers. Used by permission. All rights reserved."

Printed in Dallas, Texas by The Odee Company

Contact: contact@first15.org
www.first15.org

Designed by Matt Ravenelle
mattravenelle.com

ABOUT FIRST15

Spending time alone with God every day can be a struggle. We're busier – and more stressed – than ever. But still, we know it's important to spend time alone with our Creator. We know we need to read his word, pray, and worship him.

First15 bridges the gap between desire and reality, helping you establish the rhythm of meaningful, daily experiences in God's presence. First15 answers the critical questions:

- Why should I spend time alone with God?
- How do I spend time alone with God?
- How do I get the most out of my time alone with God?
- How can I become more consistent with my time alone with God?

And by answering these questions through the format of daily devotionals, you'll practice the rhythm of meeting with God while experiencing the incredible gift of his loving presence given to those who make time to meet with him.

Allow God's passionate pursuit to draw you in across the next several days. And watch as every day is better than the last as your life is built on the solid foundation of God's love through the power of consistent, meaningful time alone with him.

To learn more about First15, visit our website first15.org. First15 is available across mobile app, email, podcast, and our website. Subscribe to our devotional today and experience God in a fresh way every day.

ABOUT THE AUTHOR

Craig Denison is the author of First15, a daily devotional guiding over a million believers into a fresh experience with God every day. In 2015, Craig founded First15 after sensing a longing in God's heart for his people to be about relationship – real, restored relationship with him – that above all else, he simply wanted the hearts of his people. Craig began praying, dreaming, and writing. And the idea of helping people spend the first fifteen minutes of their day focusing on nothing else but growing in their relationship with God was born. The vision was birthed in Craig's heart that if we as a people would worship, read, and pray at the beginning of every day, everything could change for the better. Craig writes, speaks, and he and his wife, Rachel lead worship to help believers establish a more tangible, meaningful connection with God.

CONTENTS

Righteousness in Christ
Week 1

Light
Week 2

Renewal
Week 3

Transformation
Week 4

Day 1	Our Sin and the Holiness of God	12-15
Day 2	The Example of Moses	16-19
Day 3	The Tearing of the Veil	20-23
Day 4	An Unveiled Lifestyle	24-27
Day 5	Faith Guides Us In	28-31
Day 6	The Omnipresence of God	32-35
Day 7	Our Righteousness in Jesus Christ	36-39
Day 8	Light and Dark	46-49
Day 9	We are Called to the Light	50-53
Day 10	Jesus is the Light	54-57
Day 11	Living Fully Known	58-61
Day 12	Looking at the Light	62-65
Day 13	Following God into the Light	66-69
Day 14	Being the Light	70-73
Day 15	God's Plan for Renewal	80-83
Day 16	The Renewal of Your Mind	84-87
Day 17	Renewal of Your First Love	88-91
Day 18	Renewal of Joy	92-95
Day 19	Renewal of Purpose	96-99
Day 20	Renewal of Conscience	100-103
Day 21	Renewal of Perspective	104-107
Day 22	Seeking Transformation	114-117
Day 23	God Transforms Us Into New Creations	118-120
Day 24	Continual Transformation	122-125
Day 25	Transformation through Experience	126-129
Day 26	God Meets Us in Our Weakness	130-133
Day 27	Life in Christ	134-137
Day 28	Life in the Spirit	138-141

DAYS 1 - 7

Righteousness in Christ

01

WEEK

"For our sake he made him to be sin who knew no sin, so that in him we might become the righteousness of God."
2 Corinthians 5:21

WEEKLY OVERVIEW

Living an unveiled lifestyle is the way in which we experience the fullness of what's available to us in our restored relationship with God. It's a powerful lifestyle of faith, direct encounters with our heavenly Father, and life transformation. It's when we live our lives in light of the perfect sacrifice of Jesus that we begin to experience all his death was purposed to bring us. God longs for his children to walk in intimacy with him directly connected to his wellspring of love for us. May you experience a more tangible, loving, and powerful connection with your heavenly Father this week.

Our Sin and the Holiness of God

DAY 1

DEVOTIONAL

Our heavenly Father is both entirely full of love and completely holy. And in the greatest tragedy of all time, our sin caused the love and holiness of our God to be at opposition with one another. His greatest desire was for unadulterated, perfect relationship with us. And with Adam and Eve that longing was

> *"But he shall not go through the veil or approach the altar, because he has a blemish, that he may not profane my sanctuaries, for I am the Lord who sanctifies them."*
>
> LEVITICUS 21:23

fulfilled. He could enjoy communion with us without separation. But when sin entered the grand narrative of human history God's unshakable, holy nature could not allow him to walk in perfect communion with us any longer. Our sin caused a rift between us and him that his love could not yet overcome.

So great is the holiness of our God and so great was the depth of our sin that a veil was placed between us and our heavenly Father, a veil signifying the horrific separation of God and man. In a description of the veil, Exodus 26:31-33 says, *"And you shall make a veil of blue and purple and scarlet yarns and fine twined linen. It shall be made with cherubim skillfully worked into it. And you shall hang it on four pillars of acacia overlaid with gold, with hooks of gold, on four bases of silver. And you shall hang the veil from the clasps, and bring the ark of the testimony in there within the veil. And the veil shall separate for you the Holy Place from the Most Holy."*

Only one man, chosen to go before God as Israel's representative, was allowed to pass through the veil once a year on the Day of Atonement. And so great was God's holiness and our sin that if anyone else was to enter, the power of God's holiness would kill them. In Leviticus 16:2, God commanded Moses, *"Tell Aaron your brother not to come at any time into the Holy Place inside the veil, before the mercy seat that is on the ark, so that he may not die. For I will appear in the cloud over the mercy seat."*

In order to appreciate the power of Christ's sacrifice, we must acknowledge the status from which we have been redeemed. In Luke 7:47, in reference to the depth of a prostitute's love for him, Jesus says, *"Therefore I tell you, her sins, which are many, are forgiven—for she loved much. But he who is forgiven little, loves little."* You have been forgiven much regardless of what lifestyle you have come from. So great was the chasm your sin created that you were incapable of communion with your Creator. Without the sacrifice of Christ you would have no restored relationship with God, no Holy Spirit dwelling within you, and no grace, mercy, or total forgiveness.

So that you might greatly love your heavenly Father today, spend time in prayer focusing on the depth of your sin, which has been sacrificially redeemed by the love of Jesus Christ.

GUIDED PRAYER

1. Meditate on the depth of your inherited sin. You were, by nature, completely separated from the love of your heavenly Father.

"We all once lived in the passions of our flesh, carrying out the desires of the body and the mind, and were by nature children of wrath, like the rest of mankind." Ephesians 2:3

"For the wages of sin is death, but the free gift of God is eternal life in Christ Jesus our Lord." Romans 6:23

"For all have sinned and fall short of the glory of God." Romans 3:23

2. Take time to reflect on what your life would be like without relationship with your heavenly Father. What would it be like to be without God's grace and forgiveness? What would it be like to be without his presence for all of your days?

3. Take time to thank God for the abundance of his goodness. Worship him for his sacrifice. Love him greatly in response to the depth of your sins.

"I give you thanks, O Lord, with my whole heart; before the gods I sing your praise; I bow down toward your holy temple and give thanks to your name for your steadfast love and your faithfulness, for you have exalted above all things your name and your word. On the day I called, you answered me; my strength of soul you increased." Psalm 138:1-3

"So I have looked upon you in the sanctuary, beholding your power and glory. Because your steadfast love is better than life, my lips will praise you. So I will bless you as long as I live; in your name I will lift up my hands." Psalm 63:2-4

"The Lord is gracious and merciful, slow to anger and abounding in steadfast love. The Lord is good to all, and his mercy is over all that he has made." Psalm 145:8-9

Seeing our sin in light of God's holiness is a difficult but wonderful reminder of how greatly God has loved us. Jesus sacrificed everything when we were deserving of nothing. May you live today in response to God's unmerited favor and grace on your life.

Extended Reading: Romans 5

WEEK 1

The Example of Moses

DAY 2

DEVOTIONAL

We find in the character of Moses a man transformed by a face-to-face, unveiled encounter with the living God. Exodus 34:29-35 says:

When Moses came down from Mount Sinai, with the two tablets of the testimony in his hand as he came down from the mountain, Moses did not know that the skin of his face shone because he had been talking with God. Aaron and all the people of Israel saw Moses, and behold, the skin of his face shone, and they were afraid to come near him. But Moses called to them, and Aaron and all the leaders of the congregation returned to him, and Moses talked with them. Afterward all the people of Israel came near, and he commanded them all that the Lord had spoken with him in Mount Sinai. And when Moses had finished speaking with them, he put a veil over his face. Whenever Moses went in before the Lord to speak with him, he would remove the veil, until he came out. And when he came out and told the people of Israel what he was commanded, the people of Israel would see the face of Moses, that the skin of Moses' face was shining. And Moses would put the veil over his face again, until he went in to speak with him.

Moses serves as an important example for you and me. Moses was a man chosen to go before God on behalf of his people and relay the will and heart of God back to them. And by the life, death, and resurrection of Jesus, we are now chosen and transformed to live out the same calling. In 1 Peter 2:9 Peter declares that we are *"a chosen race, a royal*

"Moses did not know that the skin of his face shone because he had been talking with God."

EXODUS 34:29

priesthood, a holy nation, a people for his own possession, that [we] may proclaim the excellencies of him who called [us] out of darkness into his marvelous light." We are to operate in the same capacity that Moses did. We are to be children of God that bear the image of our heavenly Father and declare his grace, love, power, and goodness to a world in desperate need of relationship with him. What happened to Moses in Exodus 34 holds true for you and me today: when we meet with God we take on the image of his glory. The difference is that the glory of God now dwells internally rather than externally by the powerful sacrifice of Jesus. As Moses' face shone with the glory of God, our new nature is now meant to shine, declaring the immeasurable grace and power of Jesus' sacrifice.

Paul writes in 2 Corinthians 4:6-7, *"For God, who said, 'Let light shine out of darkness,' has shone in our hearts to give the light of the knowledge of the glory of God in the face of Jesus Christ. But we have this treasure in jars of clay, to show that the surpassing power belongs to God and not to us."* The glory of God now dwells within us. And we are to contain his glory as water in jars of clay, that we would pour out his love and grace for all to see. Just as the people of Israel saw the face of Moses and knew he had met with God, we are to meet with our heavenly Father face-to-face and be transformed by his presence for all to see. Jesus' death has paved the way for you to meet with God face to face–unveiled. Take time in prayer to see the face of God and allow him to transform you into the likeness of Jesus.

GROW

GUIDED PRAYER

1. Meditate on Exodus 34:29. Allow Scripture to stir up your desire to meet with your heavenly Father face-to-face.

"Moses did not know that the skin of his face shone because he had been talking with God." Exodus 34:29

2. Renew your mind to your new calling in Jesus. Allow Scripture to fill you with faith to encounter God unveiled.

"But you are a chosen race, a royal priesthood, a holy nation, a people for his own possession, that you may proclaim the excellencies of him who called you out of darkness into his marvelous light." 1 Peter 2:9

"Therefore, if anyone is in Christ, he is a new creation. The old has passed away; behold, the new has come." 2 Corinthians 5:17

3. Spend time meeting with your heavenly Father face-to-face. Ask him to reveal his nearness to you. Rest in his presence and allow it to lay a new foundation for you. Ask him to make you more like him. Ask him to show you how to be a reflection of his glory to the world around you today.

"For God, who said, 'Let light shine out of darkness,' has shone in our hearts to give the light of the knowledge of the glory of God in the face of Jesus Christ. But we have this treasure in jars of clay, to show that the surpassing power belongs to God and not to us." 2 Corinthians 4:6-7

May Jesus' declaration about you in Matthew 5:14-16 serve as a constant reminder of your new calling here as a child of the living God:

"You are the light of the world. A city set on a hill cannot be hidden. Nor do people light a lamp and put it under a basket, but on a stand, and it gives light to all in the house. In the same way, let your light shine before others, so that they may see your good works and give glory to your Father who is in heaven."

Extended Reading: Exodus 34

The Tearing of the Veil

DAY 3

DEVOTIONAL

Matthew 27:45-54 says, *Now from the sixth hour there was darkness over all the land until the ninth hour. And about the ninth hour Jesus cried out with a loud voice, saying, "Eli, Eli, lema sabachthani?" that is, "My God, my God, why have you forsaken me?" And some of the bystanders, hearing it, said, "This man is calling Elijah." And one of them at once ran and took a sponge, filled it with sour wine, and put it on a reed and gave it to him to drink. But the others said, "Wait, let us see whether Elijah will come to save him." And Jesus cried out again with a loud voice and yielded up his spirit. And behold, the curtain of the temple was torn in two, from top to*

"And behold, the curtain of the temple was torn in two, from top to bottom. And the earth shook, and the rocks were split."

MATTHEW 27:51

bottom. And the earth shook, and the rocks were split. The tombs also were opened. And many bodies of the saints who had fallen asleep were raised, and coming out of the tombs after his resurrection they went into the holy city and appeared to many. When the centurion and those who were with him, keeping watch over Jesus, saw the earthquake and what took place, they were filled with awe and said, "Truly this was the Son of God!"

At the death of Jesus, God turned what was the world's greatest tragedy into our greatest triumph. With every crack of the whip, the bonds that entangled you and me to the sin and darkness of this world became a little looser. And with Jesus' final breath the earth shook and the rocks split under the magnitude of the power of Christ's sacrifice. Only God could take the greatest injustice and turn it into the world's greatest good. Only God could take death and produce abundant life for all.

Out of everything that resulted from Jesus' final breath, none was more important than God's tearing of the veil. The veil that signified the necessary separation between God and man was ripped in two from top to bottom, from God down to us. The great chasm over which no man could cross was now covered by a bridge created by God's wrath poured out on Jesus. The tearing of the veil represents the very purpose for Jesus' death: that God could now once again have restored communion with his people. No matter how many or how horrendous our sins might be, Jesus' death gained victory over it all.

Just as the saints who had fallen asleep were raised at Jesus' death, you and I have been raised to newness of life. We are caught up in the glory of Jesus' life, death, and resurrection. God has made unveiled, face-to-face relationship with him available to us once again.

If God would pay the price of Jesus' death to have restored relationship with us, encountering him face-to-face must be the absolute best way for us to live. If God considers restored relationship with you worth the death of his only and blameless Son, he must place his highest value on total communion with you.

Maybe the concept of having real, tangible encounters with your heavenly Father is new to you. Maybe he feels distant. Maybe you come in and out of his presence day-to-day. Wherever you are in relation to God, know that nothing can separate you from him any longer. The death of Jesus was more powerful than any sin, lie, or belief. His death paid the entirety of your debt. There is nothing left to pay. Seek out a revelation of what it looks like to encounter your heavenly Father unveiled in prayer. May the Holy Spirit guide you into a lifestyle of continual, face-to-face, unveiled encounters with the living God.

GUIDED PRAYER

1. Meditate on the chasm that separated you from God as the result of sin. Reflecting on your status prior to salvation will give you a greater appreciation for what Jesus has done for you.

"Therefore, just as sin came into the world through one man, and death through sin, and so death spread to all men because all sinned." Romans 5:12

"Behold, the Lord's hand is not shortened, that it cannot save, or his ear dull, that it cannot hear; but your iniquities have made a separation between you and your God, and your sins have hidden his face from you so that he does not hear." Isaiah 59:1-2

2. Now meditate on the power of Jesus' sacrifice. With his death on the cross, Jesus carried you across the great chasm that separated you from your heavenly Father.

"He entered once for all into the holy places, not by means of the blood of goats and calves but by means of his own blood, thus securing an eternal redemption." Hebrews 9:12

"And behold, the curtain of the temple was torn in two, from top to bottom. And the earth shook, and the rocks were split." Matthew 27:51

3. Worship Jesus for the newness of life available to you through him. Give him thanks and praise for his love. Allow your affections to be stirred up toward him by the truth of Scripture.

"For I am sure that neither death nor life, nor angels nor rulers, nor things present nor things to come, nor powers, nor height nor depth, nor anything else in all creation, will be able to separate us from the love of God in Christ Jesus our Lord." Romans 8:38-39

"For God so loved the world, that he gave his only Son, that whoever believes in him should not perish but have eternal life." John 3:16

"The Lord is not slow to fulfill his promise as some count slowness, but is patient toward you, not wishing that any should perish, but that all should reach repentance." 2 Peter 3:9

Never doubt the grace of your heavenly Father toward you. Jesus has paid the price for every sin you will ever commit. He bore the weight of all of our sins on the cross. God poured out the entirety of his wrath over our sin on Jesus. All that's left for you to do is live out the abundant life to which you have been called. Enjoy God and glorify him in response to his great love. May you be a child of God overcome by the goodness of your Father in heaven.

Extended Reading: Matthew 27

An Unveiled Lifestyle

DAY 4

DEVOTIONAL

By the grace of God the veil that represented our sin and shame has been replaced with shameless, limitless, and face-to-face encounters with our heavenly Father. Scripture says,

Since we have such a hope, we are very bold, not like Moses, who would put a veil over his face so that the Israelites might not gaze at the outcome of what was being brought to an end. But their minds were hardened. For to this day, when they read the old covenant, that same veil remains unlifted, because only through Christ is it taken away. Yes, to this day whenever Moses is read a veil lies over their hearts. But when one turns to the Lord, the veil is removed. Now the Lord is the Spirit, and where the Spirit of the Lord is, there is freedom. And we all, with unveiled face, beholding the glory of the Lord, are being transformed into the same image from one degree of glory to another. For this comes from the Lord who is the Spirit (2 Corinthians 3:12-18).

God longs for us to live an unveiled lifestyle. He longs for us to behold his glory and be transformed into the same image: a reflection of his glorious Son, Jesus. The idea of looking like Jesus used to seem utterly impossible. How could I ever look anything like Jesus? In my sin and shame, how could I ever resemble the perfect, sinless Son of God? But God has an enjoyable and perfect process by which he transforms us. As we seek out all that God has for us in an unveiled lifestyle, God longs to renew our minds to his plans for our transformation.

2 Corinthians 3:18 makes it clear that in *"beholding the glory of the Lord"* we are transformed. Just as Moses went into the tent of meeting and came out with his face shining (Exodus 33:7-11), we are to go into our own tent of meeting and come out having met with God with unveiled face. Allow the truth of Scripture to define what spending time with God is meant to look like for you.

> *"But when one turns to the Lord, the veil is removed."*
>
> **2 CORINTHIANS 3:16**

When we spend time alone with God, the Holy Spirit longs to lead us into direct, tangible, and transformative encounters with the glory of God. Christian spirituality is all about direct connection with our heavenly Father and not about engaging in religious practices just because we feel we should. The death of Christ has made unveiled encounters with God completely available to you whenever, wherever. We enter into our tent of meeting clothed with Christ, washed completely clean of our sin by the power of his blood.

And 2 Corinthians 3:18 also makes it clear that when we see God's glory we are *"transformed into the same image,"* the image of Jesus. Genesis 1:27 says, *"So God created man in his own image, in the image of God he created him; male and female he created them."* God's intention was always for us to represent him well. When sin entered into humanity that image became grossly distorted. But through the death of Jesus and encounters with our heavenly Father that image is being restored. We can now be reflections of God to a world that is desperately searching for relationship with its Creator. We now bear the image of the one who has saved and redeemed us.

Living an unveiled lifestyle is simply encountering our heavenly Father and living our lives as a response to his love for us. Every encounter with God changes us and makes us more like him. Every taste of his presence fills us with his love and equips us to love others. To live an unveiled lifestyle is to experience the abundant life Jesus came to bring us. May you behold the glory of your heavenly Father and be a reflection of his love to a lost and dying world today.

Spend time in prayer practicing what 2 Corinthians 3 describes for us: beholding and being transformed by the glory of God.

GUIDED PRAYER

1. Meditate on the availability for you to encounter God face-to-face, unveiled.

"But when one turns to the Lord, the veil is removed." 2 Corinthians 3:16

2. Ask the Holy Spirit to lead you into the tangible presence of your heavenly Father. Ask God to make his nearness known to you.

"You will seek me and find me, when you seek me with all your heart." Jeremiah 29:13

"My presence will go with you, and I will give you rest." Exodus 33:14

3. Spend time in God's presence being transformed by his love. Ask the Holy Spirit to make you more like Jesus. Ask God to reveal himself in a way that would mold and shape you into his likeness.

"And we all, with unveiled face, beholding the glory of the Lord, are being transformed into the same image from one degree of glory to another. For this comes from the Lord who is the Spirit." 2 Corinthians 3:18

"For those whom he foreknew he also predestined to be conformed to the image of his Son, in order that he might be the firstborn among many brothers." Romans 8:29

How incredible is our God that he would make transformation such an accessible and enjoyable process. Fully letting go of our sin and shame is difficult to be sure, but the depth of grace, love, and relationship he offers us in return makes it all worthwhile. Allow God to continue to heal any areas of your life where you feel brokenness and shame. Open up your heart to him completely today in faith and allow him to create in you a new foundation of his on which you can live freely and healed.

Extended Reading: 2 Corinthians 3

Faith Guides Us In

DAY 5

DEVOTIONAL

To see the living God face-to-face is to have our spiritual eyes opened through the important practice of faith. The entirety of our relationship with God really boils down to faith. By faith we trust in him even though we haven't seen him. By faith we believe the Bible is truly his word. And it is by faith that we enter into his tangible presence where our hearts are transformed and our lives changed.

Paul prays an important prayer at the beginning of Ephesians that I believe God desires for you and me today. Ephesians 1:17-18 says, *"That the God of our Lord Jesus Christ, the Father of glory, may give you the*

*"Let us draw near with a true
heart in full assurance of faith."*

HEBREWS 10:22

Spirit of wisdom and of revelation in the knowledge of him, having the eyes of your hearts enlightened, that you may know what is the hope to which he has called you, what are the riches of his glorious inheritance in the saints." We need the eyes of our hearts enlightened. We need to develop spiritual eyes to see all that is available to us in God. We need faith to guide us into the deeper things of God.

Hebrews 10:19-23 says, *"Therefore, brothers, since we have confidence to enter the holy places by the blood of Jesus, by the new and living way that he opened for us through the curtain, that is, through his flesh, and since we have a great priest over the house of God, let us draw near with a true heart in full assurance of faith, with our hearts sprinkled clean from an evil conscience and our bodies washed with pure water. Let us hold fast the confession of our hope without wavering, for he who promised is faithful."*

God longs for us to draw near to him. He longs for us to experience him unveiled, face-to-face with the eyes of our hearts open and our hearts full of awe and wonder. The single most exciting truth of our lives is that the God of the universe, the Creator of all, can be seen and known. Spending time with him is more satisfying, entertaining, uplifting, and better than any other way our time could be spent. If we will have the faith to make time and let God move in and on our hearts, practicing faith as God's word tells us to, we will experience a reality unknown and unseen to the naked eye. We will experience the reality of heaven: God and man joined together in communion.

Faith is a gift given to those who cry out to know God. It is a gift given by the Holy Spirit in response to our desperation for relationship. If you will seek out more in your communion with your heavenly Father, he will respond with an increase of faith. He will answer your call by carrying you into the depths of his endless love where you belong—where you've always belonged.

May God grant you a *"Spirit of wisdom and revelation"* and open *"the eyes of your heart"* today as you spend time in prayer.

GUIDED PRAYER

1. Meditate on the importance of faith in seeking the face of God.

"And without faith it is impossible to please him, for whoever would draw near to God must believe that he exists and that he rewards those who seek him." Hebrews 11:6

"Let us draw near with a true heart in full assurance of faith." Hebrews 10:22

"That the God of our Lord Jesus Christ, the Father of glory, may give you the Spirit of wisdom and of revelation in the knowledge of him, having the eyes of your hearts enlightened." Ephesians 1:17-18

2. Ask God to give you an increase of faith. Ask him to open the eyes of your heart to see him. Ask him for the Spirit of wisdom of revelation in the knowledge of him. Wait on him and allow him to fill you with faith.

3. Spend time seeking the face of your heavenly Father. Rest in his presence. Allow him to show you new things about himself. Ask him how he feels about circumstances going on in your life.

"You have said, 'Seek my face.' My heart says to you, 'Your face, Lord, do I seek.'" Psalm 27:8

May we be a people that seek out the fullness of God. May we be children awed by the beauty, majesty, mystery, and love of our Father. God has more in store for us than we could ever ask or imagine if we will seek him with all of our hearts. Fight the mediocrity of this world for the higher calling of experiencing all that God longs to give you.

Extended Reading: Psalm 27

The Omnipresence of God

DAY 6

DEVOTIONAL

The presence of our God is everywhere. He moves, lives, breathes, and works all around us. Psalm 84:3 declares the extensiveness of our heavenly Father's presence in saying, *"Even the sparrow finds a home, and the swallow a nest for herself, where she may lay her young, at your altars."* Psalm 84 proclaims that even the birds of the air find their home before the altars of

> *"Even the sparrow finds a home, and the swallow a nest for herself, where she may lay her young, at your altars."*
>
> PSALM 84:3

the almighty, living God. Even the birds of the air come before God's presence as they lay their young in the canopies. The psalm begs the question: if the birds come before their Creator while simply existing here on Earth, how much more available is the presence of our heavenly Father to us, his children? How much farther does his hand reach to us who are now covered by the powerful sacrifice of our Lord Jesus Christ?

There is nowhere we can run to and escape God's reach. David writes in Psalm 139:7-12, *"Where shall I go from your Spirit? Or where shall I flee from your presence? If I ascend to heaven, you are there! If I make my bed in Sheol, you are there! If I take the wings of the morning and dwell in the uttermost parts of the sea, even there your hand shall lead me, and your right hand shall hold me. If I say, 'Surely the darkness shall cover me, and the light about me be night,' even the darkness is not dark to you; the night is bright as the day, for darkness is as light with you."* The God of all comfort, of all mercy, of all forgiveness, and of all love surrounds you right now. And as a child of God, his Spirit now dwells within you.

Prior to Jesus' death, God's people did not have constant access to the fullness of his presence. The nature of his holiness and our sin created an insurmountable crevasse between us and him. But through Jesus' death, we now have access to God's nearness any time, any place. The veil between God and us has been torn, and we can now live our lives constantly experiencing the manifest presence of our heavenly Father.

Where do you need God's presence to fill you today? Where do you need comfort, peace, or patience? Where do you need to be loved, held, liked, or wanted? Your heavenly Father is waiting to run out to meet you as the father did with the prodigal son. He's waiting to throw you a party where you are his guest of honor. He loves you, likes you, wants you, and now, he has you. There is no better experience in life than connecting directly with your heavenly Father. May you open your heart and experience all that he longs to pour out over you today as you spend time encountering him in prayer.

GUIDED PRAYER

1. Meditate on the omnipresence of God. Renew your mind to the availability of his tangible presence.

"Even the sparrow finds a home, and the swallow a nest for herself, where she may lay her young, at your altars." Psalm 84:3

"Where shall I go from your Spirit? Or where shall I flee from your presence? If I ascend to heaven, you are there! If I make my bed in Sheol, you are there! If I take the wings of the morning and dwell in the uttermost parts of the sea, even there your hand shall lead me, and your right hand shall hold me. If I say, 'Surely the darkness shall cover me, and the light about me be night,' even the darkness is not dark to you; the night is bright as the day, for darkness is as light with you." Psalm 139:7-12

2. Now ask God to fill you with the knowledge of his presence around you. Ask him to show you his face. Ask him how he feels about you and what he wants to do in, around, and through you today. Open your heart and mind to him. Tear down any walls you have built up between you and him.

3. Rest in the glorious presence of your heavenly Father. Take time to allow his presence to go deeper and deeper. Ask him to make you increasingly aware of his goodness and nearness.

"How lovely is your dwelling place, O Lord of hosts! My soul longs, yes, faints for the courts of the Lord; my heart and flesh sing for joy to the living God. Even the sparrow finds a home, and the swallow a nest for herself, where

she may lay her young, at your altars, O Lord of hosts, my King and my God. Blessed are those who dwell in your house, ever singing your praise!" Psalm 84:1-4

We are created for direct connection with our heavenly Father. Experiencing him is meant to be our lifeblood. Walking and talking with him is the absolute most important part of life. From this type of relationship with God comes purpose, ability, grace, and love for others. This connection is what fuels us to live life here fulfilled, satisfied, empowered, and open to the Holy Spirit's guidance. Fight for your relationship with God above all else. Let nothing come before time spent with your heavenly Father in experiencing his goodness. May you live, breathe, move, and work in the presence of God today.

Extended Reading: Psalm 84

Our Righteousness in Jesus Christ

DAY 7

DEVOTIONAL

2 Corinthians 5:14-21 describes one of the most powerful outcomes of Jesus' sacrifice for us on the cross. Scripture says,

For the love of Christ controls us, because we have concluded this: that one has died for all, therefore all have died; and he died for all, that those who live might no longer live for themselves but for him who for their sake died and was raised. From now on, therefore, we regard no one according to the flesh. Even though we once

> *"For our sake he made him to be sin who knew no sin, so that in him we might become the righteousness of God."*
>
> 2 CORINTHIANS 5:21

regarded Christ according to the flesh, we regard him thus no longer. Therefore, if anyone is in Christ, he is a new creation. The old has passed away; behold, the new has come. All this is from God, who through Christ reconciled us to himself and gave us the ministry of reconciliation; that is, in Christ God was reconciling the world to himself, not counting their trespasses against them, and entrusting to us the message of reconciliation. Therefore, we are ambassadors for Christ, God making his appeal through us. We implore you on behalf of Christ, be reconciled to God. For our sake he made him to be sin who knew no sin, so that in him we might become the righteousness of God.

Jesus' death on the cross defeated the power of sin and darkness and set us free to walk in the glorious light of righteousness. You and I have been transformed by the power of Jesus' death. He took every sin we would ever commit and bore the entirety of their penalty. Through the death of Jesus, you and I are now free to live as new creations formed in the righteous and holy image of our heavenly Father.

When God tore the veil, he demonstrated that our sin and depravity couldn't hold back his presence any longer. Thousands of years of pent-up longing for restored relationship burst forth proclaiming the newfound nature of God's people who would choose to accept and follow Jesus.

There is no more important way to end this week of pursuing a greater connection to our heavenly Father than accepting our new standing before God. Even though Jesus defeated the power of sin in our lives, our great enemy continues to tempt us, lie to us, and steal from us the abundant life God intends. He continues to try to rob God of what he so fully deserves: unencumbered relationship with his children.

Satan lies to us and tells us that sin still causes God to withhold himself from us. We allow condemnation that is not of God to creep in and cause us to believe that our heavenly Father doesn't want to be with us. But the truth is, God always wants to be with his children. God runs out to us, calls us his beloved, wraps us with honor and his righteousness, and leads us into his glorious embrace.

Take time and renew your mind to your righteousness in Jesus. Ask the Spirit for fresh revelation of your freedom from sin and allow your longings to be satisfied in God rather than the world today.

GUIDED PRAYER

1. Meditate on your new nature given to you in Christ. Receive a new perspective for yourself and your relationship with God.

"For our sake he made him to be sin who knew no sin, so that in him we might become the righteousness of God." 2 Corinthians 5:21

"Therefore, if anyone is in Christ, he is a new creation. The old has passed away; behold, the new has come." 2 Corinthians 5:17

2. Confess any sin or lie that has been keeping you from walking in the fullness of what's available to you with your heavenly Father.

"If we confess our sins, he is faithful and just to forgive us our sins and to cleanse us from all unrighteousness." 1 John 1:9

3. Spend time taking your longings before God and asking him to satisfy them. What desire is burning within you? Do you long for intimacy, purpose, or friendship? Do you long to make an impact or to be enjoyed? Come before God and spend time allowing him to love you, fill you, empower you, and satisfy you.

Praise God that he is a loving Father who loves to be with and satisfy the needs of his children! God longs for us to bring to him all our problems, insecurities, sin, and shame so he can cover them to overflowing with his merciful love. May you find rest, satisfaction, and healing in the arms of your heavenly Father today.

Extended Reading: 2 Corinthians 5

DAYS 8 - 14

Light

02

WEEK

"The light shines in the darkness, and the darkness has not overcome it."
John 1:5

WEEKLY OVERVIEW

We live in the reality that there is both light and darkness around us at all times. This world has both good and evil, right and wrong. As believers we must grow in both our acceptance of this reality and our pursuit of the light. We must allow God to mold and shape us into those who rid ourselves of any darkness, become fully known to God, and allow his light to transform us into reflections of his Son. May the Lord open our eyes to see the glorious light before us this week.

Light and Dark

DAY 8

DEVOTIONAL

All throughout Scripture God reiterates a consistent, powerful metaphor: light and dark. Scripture depicts the darkness as that which is without God and light as that which has God in it. As *"children of light,"* it's vital for us to dive deeply into this concept of light and dark that we might experience the fullness of all God has made available to us (1 Thessalonians 5:5). We must accept that both light and dark exist, that we can engage with both, and learn what it is to choose light at every turn.

In Isaiah 42:16 God says, *"I will lead the blind in a way that they do not know, in paths that they have not known I will guide them. I will turn the darkness before*

> *"For anything that becomes visible is light. Therefore it says, 'Awake, O sleeper, and arise from the dead, and Christ will shine on you.'"*
>
> **EPHESIANS 5:14**

them into light, the rough places into level ground. These are the things I do, and I do not forsake them." God has not left us to wander in darkness. He never leaves us or forsakes us (Deuteronomy 31:6). We who were blind to the paths of God have had our eyes opened through the powerful sacrifice of Jesus. We now have relationship with the Holy Spirit who seeks to guide us into the light with every thought, emotion, action, and decision.

Ephesians 5:14 says, *"For anything that becomes visible is light. Therefore it says, 'Awake, O sleeper, and arise from the dead, and Christ will shine on you.'"* It's time for you and me to arise from any part of darkness and live in the shining light of Christ Jesus. It's time for us to wake up from our former lives that were consumed with chaos, lies, and sin, come out of the shadows, and find true life in the light of God's presence, will, and word.

God has so much more in store for you than a life lived working to escape darkness. The power of Jesus' sacrifice has hidden you in him. His light is your light. But before we can experience this fullness of life available to us, we must allow him to open our eyes. We must allow him into the darkest places of our past, thoughts, feelings, and perspectives. We must allow his light to illuminate our darkest of sins in order that those which cause us the most shame might be healed and broken off of our lives.

Just as light can hurt a little at first when we've become accustomed to darkness, seeing the parts of our lives that we've shut off to God, others, and even ourselves can be painful. But, once we've allowed God to illuminate our whole lives that we might see ourselves as we truly are, we will discover a wealth of grace, love, and forgiveness unlike any we've ever known. Once we experience the unconditional love of a God who knows all we've ever done, thought, and felt, our lives begin to change by his overwhelming goodness. Light is powerful in its ability to heal, set free, and empower.

Take time in guided prayer to open your heart to your heavenly Father and reflect on this biblical principle of light and dark. Allow Scripture to fill you with a desire to seek the light of God in all things. Ask the Holy Spirit to illuminate the places in your life he longs to heal. And find grace, rest, and forgiveness in the loving presence of your heavenly Father.

GUIDED PRAYER

1. Meditate on this biblical metaphor of light and dark. Reflect on the truth of Scripture that your mind would be renewed to the reality of the choice before you to live in the light.

"The people dwelling in darkness have seen a great light, and for those dwelling in the region and shadow of death, on them a light has dawned." Matthew 4:16

"And I will lead the blind in a way that they do not know, in paths that they have not known I will guide them. I will turn the darkness before them into light, the rough places into level ground. These are the things I do, and I do not forsake them." Isaiah 42:16

"For anything that becomes visible is light. Therefore it says, 'Awake, O sleeper, and arise from the dead, and Christ will shine on you.'" Ephesians 5:14

2. What areas of your life have yet to be fully illuminated, healed, set free, and empowered by God? Where do you need God's grace, truth, and help in choosing light over darkness?

"For at one time you were darkness, but now you are light in the Lord. Walk as children of light." Ephesians 5:8

"The spirit of man is the lamp of the Lord, searching all his innermost parts." Proverbs 20:27

3. Ask God to show you how he feels about the dark places in your life. Ask him to speak truth to your areas of need. Ask his forgiveness for any ways in which you've been living in darkness.

"But if we walk in the light, as he is in the light, we have fellowship with one another, and the blood of Jesus his Son cleanses us from all sin." 1 John 1:7

"But you are a chosen race, a royal priesthood, a holy nation, a people for his own possession, that you may proclaim the excellencies of him who called you out of darkness into his marvelous light." 1 Peter 2:9

The fullness of life is only available in the light. Anything we experience in darkness is a mere shadow of what is available to us with God. Any pleasure we find in impurity, lies, and pride is nothing compared to the inexhaustible satisfaction available in God's light. Trust God that he absolutely has the best life in store for you if you choose him. Trust him that the fullness of joy, peace, purpose, and pleasure is found in him alone. May your day be filled with the peace and joy that comes from living in the light of God.

Extended Reading: Ephesians 5

We are Called to the Light

DAY 9

DEVOTIONAL

In Colossians 1:11-14, Paul prays a powerful prayer in his letter to the church in Colossae, and I believe it's God's heart for you and me today. Scripture says,

May you be strengthened with all power, according to his glorious might, for all endurance and patience with joy, giving thanks to the Father, who has qualified you to share in the

> *"For at one time you were darkness, but now you are light in the Lord. Walk as children of light."*
>
> **EPHESIANS 5:8**

inheritance of the saints in light. He has delivered us from the domain of darkness and transferred us to the kingdom of his beloved Son, in whom we have redemption, the forgiveness of sins.

You and I have been redeemed from living bound to darkness and have been given a new name, *"saints in light."* We've been delivered from the dark things of this world that previously defined us and ushered into a new kingdom filled with the light of God.

Ephesians 5:8 says, *"For at one time you were darkness, but now you are light in the Lord. Walk as children of light."* As *"children of light,"* we must learn to walk in our new inheritance. We must learn what it is to be disciples marked by the characteristics of our Father's kingdom. The powerful sacrifice of Jesus has afforded us an opportunity to no longer live as those of the world. We belong to a kingdom that stretches past the span of this life through the unending reach of eternity. God's kingdom will have no end. His goodness and mercies will never cease. A relationship founded on the good, pleasing principles of his kingdom is eternal.

But while we live on this earth we will experience temptations, trials, and doubts that continually try to pull us out of our new life of eternal inheritance and back into the fleeting ways and pursuits of darkness. We must learn to look past this world and reject that which calls us back to the dark. We must learn to look past the pleasures, glory, possessions, and accolades available to us here and find our satisfaction in the things of God alone.

You have been called by the One True God a *"[saint] in light."* You have been ransomed from that which won't last and brought into the eternal goodness of God's kingdom. In Matthew 6:33, Jesus says, *"But seek first the kingdom of God and his righteousness, and all these things will be added to you."* All that you desire finds its true fulfillment in the light. All the purpose, joy, passion, pleasure, and provision you seek will be fully satisfied in God if you seek his kingdom first. Turn your life away from anything resembling darkness and commit yourself to living in the light. May God grant you the grace and mercy to seek his kingdom at every turn today that you might know the unfathomable excellencies of unhindered relationship with him.

GUIDED PRAYER

1. Meditate on your calling to live in the light. Allow Scripture to fill you with perspective on what it is to walk in the light.

"For at one time you were darkness, but now you are light in the Lord. Walk as children of light." Ephesians 5:8

"You are the light of the world. A city set on a hill cannot be hidden." Matthew 5:14

"But you are a chosen race, a royal priesthood, a holy nation, a people for his own possession, that you may proclaim the excellencies of him who called you out of darkness into his marvelous light." 1 Peter 2:9

2. What desires are you satisfying in darkness rather than light? Ask God to show you ways in which he wants to satisfy those desires to an even greater measure.

3. Take time to receive God's presence and be filled with his Spirit. Enjoy the light of God's love, peace, and goodness. Find satisfaction in who he is and how deeply he cares for you.

"May you be strengthened with all power, according to his glorious might, for all endurance and patience with joy, giving thanks to the Father, who has qualified you to share in the inheritance of the saints in light. He has delivered us from the domain of darkness and transferred us to the kingdom of his beloved Son, in whom we have redemption, the forgiveness of sins." Colossians 1:11-14

We're not often told of the wonderful satisfaction available to us in God. So much of our faith is based on rules, regulations, and "don'ts" rather than the wealth of life God longs to give us in his kingdom. All God desires us to do or not do is based on his passion for blessing us. All God would lead us away from or into is for the sole purpose of our good. He is not a self-seeking God. He is not a taskmaster. He is a good Father who desires to abundantly bless his children. Life with God is a life filled with the fullness of satisfaction. May you experience the abundant blessing that can only be found in the light of God today.

Extended Reading: 1 Peter 1

Jesus is the Light

DAY 10

DEVOTIONAL

To live in the light is to center our lives wholly around its only true source: Jesus. Jesus powerfully declares in John 8:12, *"I am the light of the world. Whoever follows me will not walk in darkness, but will have the light of life."* As those committed to following Jesus, we are constantly being led by him into the light. He is constantly beckoning us away from the darkness of this world and calling us to a life centered around him and his kingdom.

> *"Your sun shall no more go down, nor your moon withdraw itself; for the Lord will be your everlasting light, and your days of mourning shall be ended."*
>
> **ISAIAH 60:20**

In and of ourselves, we have no light. Left to our own devices, we would live our entire lives in darkness, void of the abundance of joy and peace available to us in God. But through Jesus the light has come. The Holy Spirit now dwells within us, the glory of God in the hearts of men. If we will simply surrender our lives to God and the light he brings, we will experience a life of freedom and joy founded in his unconditional love. If we will choose to place Jesus at the center of all we do and who we are, we will receive mighty deliverance from the constraints and bonds of darkness.

You see, the path out of darkness always begins by looking to the light. We can't escape darkness if darkness is all we're looking toward. We can't escape sin by just focusing on it and trying to fix it, heal it, or set ourselves free. Freedom comes by turning our attention to the God who conquered sin and death and fixing our eyes on Jesus, the author and perfecter of our faith.

2 Corinthians 4:6 says, *"For God, who said, 'Let light shine out of darkness,' has shone in our hearts to give the light of the knowledge of the glory of God in the face of Jesus Christ."* The light of God is within you. Your life as a Christian is hidden in Christ. The darkness will not overcome you. Your freedom has come in the person of Jesus. The love of God is real, available, and powerful enough to set you free from whatever darkness entangles you.

Turn your attention fully toward Jesus today. Center your life around his loving-kindness. Open your ears and heart to this good God who would lay down his life to save yours. Follow him wherever he guides you in full faith that he will only ever lead you into more abundant life. Cease striving for your own freedom and wrap your life up in Jesus that he might be your great deliverer, healer, and source of comfort and strength.

God has abundant grace in store for you today if you will simply position yourself to receive it. Take time in guided prayer to reflect on the light that has come through Jesus, turn your attention completely toward him, and receive the freedom and healing that comes from union with the God of light.

GUIDED PRAYER

1. Meditate on the light that has come through Jesus. Allow Scripture to stir up your desire to truly open your heart and center your life around Jesus.

"I am the light of the world. Whoever follows me will not walk in darkness, but will have the light of life." John 8:12

"For God, who said, 'Let light shine out of darkness,' has shone in our hearts to give the light of the knowledge of the glory of God in the face of Jesus Christ." 2 Corinthians 4:6

"In this the love of God was made manifest among us, that God sent his only Son into the world, so that we might live through him." 1 John 4:9

2. Turn your heart completely toward Jesus and focus your attention on him. Ask the Holy Spirit to guide you into an encounter with your Savior.

3. Talk with Jesus about any areas in your life that seem to have darkness. Lay down any sin and darkness at his feet and ask for his forgiveness and healing. Ask the Spirit to help you follow him as he leads you out of the darkness and into the light by focusing on Jesus.

"Therefore, since we are surrounded by so great a cloud of witnesses, let us also lay aside every weight, and sin which clings so closely, and let us run with endurance the race that is set before us, looking to Jesus, the founder and perfecter of our faith, who for the joy that was set before him endured the cross, despising the shame, and is seated at the right hand of the throne of God." Hebrews 12:1-2

"Your sun shall no more go down, nor your moon withdraw itself; for the Lord will be your everlasting light, and your days of mourning shall be ended." Isaiah 60:20

"The Lord is my light and my salvation; whom shall I fear? The Lord is the stronghold of my life; of whom shall I be afraid?" Psalm 27:1

There is most definitely a place in freedom for discipline and the practicalities of stepping away from that which normally tempts you. But the foundation for freedom will always be encounters with the living God. There is a reason we sin that goes past the temptation to a wound, misconception, or lie that must be healed by God. To not place ourselves in situations that have habitually caused us to stumble is crucial, but it will not provide healing. Look to Jesus today. Come to him continually with your sin and ask him to heal whatever is the root of it. Ask him to correct any lies and heal your pain. May you experience freedom today that comes from seeking the light of Jesus.

Extended Reading: 1 John 4

Living Fully Known

DAY 11

DEVOTIONAL

To live in secrecy before God, man, and yourself is to live in darkness. We are made to be fully known. We are made to be open and vulnerable. It's only in the place of living fully known that we can truly receive the depths of God's love for us. It's only in being fully known that we discover who we really are and the immensity of our need for God.

> *"For nothing is hidden that will not be made manifest, nor is anything secret that will not be known and come to light."*
>
> **LUKE 8:17**

Our culture values perception above reality. We work tirelessly to create an image of perfection in the minds of others that requires a constant covering-up of who we truly are. We work to build up a facade, a false outer shell, in attempts to keep in darkness that which we fear will cause rejection. But the greater our facade the less we are truly loved. When someone loves an image we've created that we know isn't truly us, we can't receive that love. When someone compliments the image of perfection we've worked to create, we are all the time thinking, "If you only knew who I really was, you wouldn't be saying those things." To be fully loved is to be fully known.

The sobering truth of Scripture is that God already knows the secrets of our heart and will one day bring them out into the light whether we desire it or not. Hebrews 4:13 says, *"And no creature is hidden from his sight, but all are naked and exposed to the eyes of him to whom we must give account."* Luke 8:17 says, *"For nothing is hidden that will not be made manifest, nor is anything secret that will not be known and come to light."* God knows the importance of everything being brought to the light. His chief desire is full relationship with us, and he knows full relationship only occurs without secrets.

While God knows the secrets of our heart already, we will not receive the fullness of his love here on earth until we willingly open them up to him. God patiently waits for us to make ourselves fully known to him, all the while beckoning us with his loving-kindness. He declares his good nature to us through Scripture, circumstances, and his Spirit, knocking on the door of our hearts that we might let him in to love us, heal us, and set us free.

Take time today to open your life to God, and with his help, tear down whatever facade you've built up. Engage in the process of living fully known by offering up the parts of your heart you've never wanted to bring to the light. Tell him of your secrets. Make some space to reflect on your life. What do you work tirelessly to keep in the dark? What thoughts, motives, or wounds do you constantly try and hide? Trust that your God is a good Father. He already knows the secrets of your life. He will not reject you. He is not disgusted with or ashamed of you. He simply wants to fully love you. May you experience the love of your heavenly Father to greater measures today as you seek to live fully known.

GUIDED PRAYER

1. Meditate on the importance of being fully known. Take time to reflect on your life and what living with a facade does to your heart. Think about the wonders of being both fully known and fully loved.

"For nothing is hidden that will not be made manifest, nor is anything secret that will not be known and come to light." Luke 8:17

"And no creature is hidden from his sight, but all are naked and exposed to the eyes of him to whom we must give account." Hebrews 4:13

2. What secrets, wounds, motives, or thoughts are in darkness? What do you work tirelessly to conceal from others? What are you even working to hide from yourself?

3. Tell God about what you've hidden in darkness. Journal, pray, or reflect with him about that which you've tried to hide. Open up to him and ask him how he feels about you. Ask him how he feels about what you've kept hidden. Take time and simply let him love and enjoy you.

"No, in all these things we are more than conquerors through him who loved us. For I am sure that neither death nor life, nor angels nor rulers, nor things present nor things to come, nor powers, nor height nor depth, nor anything else in all creation, will be able to separate us from the love of God in Christ Jesus our Lord." Romans 8:37-39

There is something so powerful about simply being enjoyed by God. When we find that he delights in us, everything changes. In the fifth century, St. Augustine said, "Quia amasti me, fecisti me amabilem," which means, "In loving me, you made me lovable." To experience the love of God is to learn that apart from anything we could ever do, we are lovable. You are lovable just as you are, and you can never become unlovable. The God who alone sees every part of you and who alone is true loves you just as you are. May you find security, joy, and peace in the relentless love of your heavenly Father.

Extended Reading: Psalm 36

Looking at the Light

DAY 12

DEVOTIONAL

We live in a world filled with darkness of all forms. On any given day we are inundated with temptation after temptation, lie after lie, darkness after darkness. But in the person of Jesus a powerful hope has entered into the story of humanity. Matthew 4:16 says, *"The people dwelling in darkness have seen a great light, and for those dwelling in the region and shadow of death, on them a light has dawned."* You and I now have

> *"Your eye is the lamp of your body. When your eye is healthy, your whole body is full of light, but when it is bad, your body is full of darkness."*

LUKE 11:34

the choice to fill our lives with the light of God. We're delivered from a life marked by darkness and set free to fill ourselves with the things of God.

But still, there is a choice set before us. The light has come, but we have a real enemy trying to draw us back to the darkness at every turn. It's for this reason Jesus said in Luke 11:34, *"Your eye is the lamp of your body. When your eye is healthy, your whole body is full of light, but when it is bad, your body is full of darkness."* You and I must choose to look to the light if we want to be spiritually healthy and full of light. We must look to the light if we want the abundant life God offers us throughout every season of this life.

Paul writes in Philippians 4:8, *"Finally, brothers, whatever is true, whatever is honorable, whatever is just, whatever is pure, whatever is lovely, whatever is commendable, if there is any excellence, if there is anything worthy of praise, think about these things."* I pray that God would train us to look upon only that which will fill us with more of him. I pray that he would train our minds to think about only that which will truly satisfy the deep desires of our hearts.

Darkness is often only tempting to look at because we have yet to experience the immense satisfaction found in the light. So often God is characterized as a taskmaster out to ruin all the fun. And so often our church services, speech, and lives depict our Father as anyone but a fun, satisfying God. But if we will take some time to trust the truth of Scripture and get to know our heavenly Father as a friend, we will discover a wellspring of life to which no darkness could ever compare. The pleasures of the enemy are nothing but a shadow of the satisfaction we have in the light. Lust, adultery, earthly glory, the opinion of man, and pride in possessions are nothing compared to total, open, and eternal relationship with a good, near, and loving God.

Look to the light today for all you need. Cultivate a hunger and thirst for the things of God that can only be quenched in relationship with your heavenly Father. Run to God with your temptations, needs, and desires and ask him to lead you to satisfaction. And open your heart to him today that you might receive a wealth of love, purpose, joy, affection, and enjoyment from the only true source of life in this earth.

GUIDED PRAYER

1. Meditate on the importance of looking to the light. Allow Scripture to fill you with a desire to spend your day out of the darkness and in the light.

"Your eye is the lamp of your body. When your eye is healthy, your whole body is full of light, but when it is bad, your body is full of darkness." Luke 11:34

"If we say we have fellowship with him while we walk in darkness, we lie and do not practice the truth. But if we walk in the light, as he is in the light, we have fellowship with one another, and the blood of Jesus his Son cleanses us from all sin." 1 John 1:6-7

2. What darkness do you normally look to? Where are you running to satisfy desires that should be met in God? In what ways do you not trust that he will satisfy the needs of your heart?

3. Go to God with whatever needs you have and ask him to reveal the ways in which he wants to satisfy them. Take time to wait on him, press into his heart, and receive the wealth of his affections for you.

"Your sun shall no more go down, nor your moon withdraw itself; for the Lord will be your everlasting light, and your days of mourning shall be ended." Isaiah 60:20

At times, the desires we feel are wrong desires that God cannot satisfy. However, these wrong desires are always indicative of a deeper desire that God does want to satisfy. Lust and adultery are desires indicative of a need to be loved, liked, seen as beautiful or handsome, or simply enjoyed. Wrongful ambition and glory-seeking are wrong desires indicative of a true need to have passion and make a deep and lasting impact on the earth. The temptations of the enemy and satisfactions we find in darkness are mere shadows compared to the true satisfaction available in God. Discover the root of your wrongful desires. Ask the Holy Spirit to reveal the true needs within your heart and to guide you to a lifestyle of fulfillment in God. May your eyes be wholly focused on the light today as you seek fulfillment in your heavenly Father.

Extended Reading: Isaiah 60

Following God into the Light

DAY 13

DEVOTIONAL

The Holy Spirit dwelling within is always leading us out of darkness and into the light. He is ready and available to guide us through every decision, temptation, trial, tribulation, and circumstance that we might experience all the abundance available to us in his light.

> *"And I will lead the blind in a way that they do not know, in paths that they have not known I will guide them. I will turn the darkness before them into light, the rough places into level ground. These are the things I do, and I do not forsake them."*
>
> **ISAIAH 42:16**

God promises us in Isaiah 42:16, *"And I will lead the blind in a way that they do not know, in paths that they have not known I will guide them. I will turn the darkness before them into light, the rough places into level ground. These are the things I do, and I do not forsake them."* You serve a loving, good Father who doesn't leave you to figure out life on your own. He doesn't even leave you just with Scripture to find your way into the light. He knows that we are blind without him. He knows that we are in immense need of his help. And he is constantly leading us into the better things he has for us.

1 Corinthians 10:13 encourages us that, *"No temptation has overtaken you that is not common to man. God is faithful, and he will not let you be tempted beyond your ability, but with the temptation he will also provide the way of escape, that you may be able to endure it."* With every temptation the enemy brings, God is leading us in a great escape. You and I so often don't know the way out of temptation. It feels impossible to find the path to righteousness when all we feel is wrongful desire welling up within us. But if we will acknowledge that we are indeed blind and reach out our arms for the guiding hand of God, he *"will turn the darkness before [us] into light"* (Isaiah 42:16). He is our faithful Shepherd to the abundant pastures available to us on the other side of temptation.

Hebrews 2:18 says, *"For because he himself has suffered when tempted, he is able to help those who are being tempted."* Our God is compassionate because he has felt the temptations we feel. He has walked through this life and lived in the light. You are not alone in your sin. You are not alone in your temptations. You are not alone in the trials, decisions, and circumstances that seem to draw you into darkness. Your Savior has compassion on you and longs for you to simply lean on his strength, trust him, and follow him.

"He who is in you is greater than he who is in the world" (1 John 4:4). You will overcome your enemy if you reach out for the help of God. He will lead you away from the sin that entangles you and direct you to his perfect, peaceful paths of righteousness. Have faith in the love and ability of your God and follow him throughout your day to the still, calm waters of his presence.

GUIDED PRAYER

1. Meditate on God's desire and ability to lead you into the light. Allow Scripture to stir up your faith to follow God in the midst of trials, circumstances, and temptations.

"And I will lead the blind in a way that they do not know, in paths that they have not known I will guide them. I will turn the darkness before them into light, the rough places into level ground. These are the things I do, and I do not forsake them." Isaiah 42:16

"No temptation has overtaken you that is not common to man. God is faithful, and he will not let you be tempted beyond your ability, but with the temptation he will also provide the way of escape, that you may be able to endure it." 1 Corinthians 10:13

2. What temptations seem to envelop you where you feel no way out? What wrongful desires do you not seem to be able to get rid of?

3. Ask God how he is leading you away from those temptations. Ask him to help you reach for his help in the midst of darkness that you might follow him to the light. Take time to reflect on and journal the ways in which he will lead you to the light.

"For because he himself has suffered when tempted, he is able to help those who are being tempted." Hebrews 2:18

May Psalm 23:1-6 fill your heart with a longing for close, open relationship with your good Shepherd today as you seek to live in the light:

The Lord is my shepherd; I shall not want. He makes me lie down in green pastures. He leads me beside still waters. He restores my soul. He leads me in paths of righteousness for his name's sake. Even though I walk through the valley of the shadow of death, I will fear no evil, for you are with me; your rod and your staff, they comfort me. You prepare a table before me in the presence of my enemies; you anoint my head with oil; my cup overflows.

Extended Reading: Hebrews 2

DEVOTIONAL

The heart of our heavenly Father is to partner with us in seeing the light of his kingdom advance to every dark corner of the earth. Why he in his perfect wisdom has chosen to use us baffles me. But his desire to co-labor with us is the truth of Scripture. God has called us to be the light shining into the darkness of others' lives in love.

> *"You are the light of the world. A city set on a hill cannot be hidden."*
>
> **MATTHEW 5:14**

Jesus said it this way in Matthew 5:14-16,

You are the light of the world. A city set on a hill cannot be hidden. Nor do people light a lamp and put it under a basket, but on a stand, and it gives light to all in the house. In the same way, let your light shine before others, so that they may see your good works and give glory to your Father who is in heaven.

For a long time I considered myself incapable of giving *"light to all in the house."* I know my weaknesses all too well. I see the darkness in my life. How can I give light to anyone? You see, I thought the light I was supposed to give was the light of my own perfection. I thought I needed to get my life sorted out before I could ever minister to someone else. And out of that misconception I failed to experience the abundant life that comes from being used by God.

The truth of Scripture is that God is not calling us to minister out of our perfection. He isn't calling us to figure everything out before we can be used. The most powerful declaration we can make to those in darkness is that we who are in desperate need have been met by a perfectly loving Savior. When all the world sees is our facade of perfection, they know right away that they don't belong in Christianity. But when we live with the courage to be truly vulnerable and honest, we open our lives for those in darkness to see the light of God within us—that he in his grace encounters, loves, and dwells with weak and desperate men and women.

God is not calling you to share with the world your own perfection. He is calling you to simply be who you truly are, encounter his loving-kindness, and share with the world the grace-filled hope we have in Christ. Take time today to simply let God love you. Allow him to mold and shape you into a child who wholly experiences the love of the Father. And from that place of being loved as you are, open up your life and love others as you have been loved. Live today openly and honestly before God and man. Open up your life to those in darkness that they might see the light of God's glorious grace. And live as the light of the world, illuminating the path to God's heart for all those around you. May you experience the joy, passion, and purpose that comes from being used by God to advance his kingdom today.

GUIDED PRAYER

1. Meditate on your calling to be the light of the world. Remember that all God desires from you today is to be open and honest before him and others. He simply wants you to be loved and to love.

"But he said to me, 'My grace is sufficient for you, for my power is made perfect in weakness.' Therefore I will boast all the more gladly of my weaknesses, so that the power of Christ may rest upon me." 2 Corinthians 12:9

"All authority in heaven and on earth has been given to me. Go therefore and make disciples of all nations, baptizing them in the name of the Father and of the Son and of the Holy Spirit, teaching them to observe all that I have commanded you. And behold, I am with you always, to the end of the age." Matthew 28:18-20

"You are the light of the world. A city set on a hill cannot be hidden. Nor do people light a lamp and put it under a basket, but on a stand, and it gives light to all in the house. In the same way, let your light shine before others, so that they may see your good works and give glory to your Father who is in heaven." Matthew 5:14-16

2. Take time to simply let God love you. Open your heart and draw near to him with confidence. Rest in his presence. Ask him how he feels about you. Experience his love today.

"So we have come to know and to believe the love that God has for us. God is love, and whoever abides in love abides in God, and God abides in him." 1 John 4:16

"But God shows his love for us in that while we were still sinners, Christ died for us." Romans 5:8

"There is no fear in love, but perfect love casts out fear. For fear has to do with punishment, and whoever fears has not been perfected in love." 1 John 4:18

3. Ask the Holy Spirit how he wants to use you to be the light of the world today. Whom can you be open and honest with about who God is and what he has done in your life? Whom can you love well today?

"We love because he first loved us. If anyone says, 'I love God,' and hates his brother, he is a liar; for he who does

not love his brother whom he has seen cannot love God whom he has not seen. And this commandment we have from him: whoever loves God must also love his brother." 1 John 4:19-21

"For you are all children of light, children of the day. We are not of the night or of the darkness." 1 Thessalonians 5:5

"For at one time you were darkness, but now you are light in the Lord. Walk as children of light." Ephesians 5:8

You are already the light of the world just as you are. God has called you that from the moment of your salvation. Your light doesn't depend on what you did yesterday or the thought you just had. You are the light because God dwells within you and is constantly beckoning you to let him work through you. You are the light because you have been redeemed and your life is hidden in Christ. You are the light because he has told you so. Live with faith in what God has spoken over your life. Look for opportunities to see his word spoken over you come to fruition. And work in union with him allowing him to anoint all you do. May those in darkness come to the light as the result of Christ working in you and through you today.

Extended Reading: James 2

DAYS 15 - 21

Renewal

03

"Let us know; let us press on to know the Lord; his going out is sure as the dawn; he will come to us as the showers, as the spring rains that water the earth." Hosea 6:3

WEEKLY OVERVIEW

One of the best aspects of spending time alone with God is being renewed daily by his word and presence. When we make space for God in our lives, especially at the beginning of the day, he is faithful to renew and prepare us for all we will face out in the world. Scripture says, *"The steadfast love of the Lord never ceases; his mercies never come to an end; they are new every morning; great is your faithfulness"* (Lamentations 3:22-23). Where do you need renewal? How greatly do you need God's mercies in your life? He has a plan this week to both teach and guide you into an encounter with him that will renew you with his overwhelming goodness and love. Make space for God. Make time to encounter him. And experience the refreshing spring rain he longs to bring to heal the dry and weary places of your heart.

God's Plan for Renewal

DAY 15

DEVOTIONAL

God has an incredible plan for renewal in your life. He knows better than anyone the trials, circumstances, and people that wear you down. And he knows that you need time to be refreshed by him. Often, we seek rest and renewal from people and entertainment. Our friends, family, and entertainment can be great sources of fun and rest to be sure, but the only consistent and true source of renewal we have is spending time with our heavenly Father. Only he knows to the full extent what you need. And only he can give it to you. So, before we dive into the process of having specific areas of our lives renewed by God this week, let's allow him to simply reveal how to rest in his word and presence.

First, let's look at what Scripture says about our need for renewal. 2 Corinthians 4:16 says, *"Though our outer self is wasting away, our inner self is being renewed day by day."* Because of the nature of sin and separation from God, we as humans will not live in our fleshly bodies forever. Genesis 3:19 says, *"By the sweat of your face you shall eat bread, till you return to the ground, for out of it you were taken; for you are dust, and to dust you shall return."* But we also have the promise of Jesus in John 11:26 that *"everyone who lives and believes in [him] shall never die."* We live on the earth knowing one day our earthly bodies will pass away, and we will at the same time be taken from this world to the next. But God's desire is that while you are here in this body you would be renewed in your spirit every day. Though your body will grow weary, he desires to strengthen your spirit with the hope of an everlasting life with an all-loving God who cares for you. You can meet with God every day. You've been given the ability through the Spirit to rest in God's presence, to know his nearness and love. You can have the same experience as Paul in being *"renewed day by day"* (2 Corinthians 4:16).

"Though our outer self is wasting away, our inner self is being renewed day by day."

2 CORINTHIANS 4:16

So, how can we experience God's promised renewal? How do we rest in God's presence and allow him to revive us? First, it starts with trusting that God will reveal his love to you when you meet with him. In Jesus' high priestly prayer in John 17, he asks God to love us with the same love with which he loves Jesus (John 17:26). When you ask him to show you his love, he will. When you make space to encounter him, he will fill you with his presence. Trust that God loves to meet with you and renew you.

Also, foundational to experiencing renewal is engaging in worship. You and I are created to worship. It is both our highest goal and greatest success. When you engage in worship daily, you will experience a renewed sense of purpose and direction. Last, spend time reading God's word, allowing it to change you and lead you to obedience.

You must experience renewal in areas of your life that are not aligned with God's word. You have to spend time allowing yourself to be shaped and transformed by what God says is best for you. So much of being renewed by God is choosing to believe his word over our experience of what we feel is true.

Let your faith be stirred to encounter your heavenly Father today. You can earnestly desire to meet with him without any fear or reservation that you won't experience his renewal. Know that when you wake up every morning, God has a plan for the time you spend with him and the ability to reveal it to you through the Holy Spirit. God earnestly desires to renew you this week. He longs to heal the wounded and dry places in your life. Spend time today meditating on God's promise of renewal, and allow your desires to be stirred to receive all that your heavenly Father longs to give you.

GUIDED PRAYER

1. Meditate on God's promise for renewal.

"The steadfast love of the Lord never ceases; his mercies never come to an end; they are new every morning; great is your faithfulness." Lamentations 3:22-23

"So we do not lose heart. Though our outer self is wasting away, our inner self is being renewed day by day. For this light momentary affliction is preparing for us an eternal weight of glory beyond all comparison, as we look not to the things that are seen but to the things that are unseen. For the things that are seen are transient, but the things that are unseen are eternal." 2 Corinthians 4:16-18

2. Reflect on areas in your life that seem dry or weary. Where do you need to be renewed today?

3. Rest in God's presence and allow his love to renew those areas of your life. Spend time in his presence. Spend time worshiping. Ask the Holy Spirit to reveal to you God's specific plan for renewal in your life. Look up Scripture that applies and let it mold and renew you.

"So we have come to know and to believe the love that God has for us. God is love, and whoever abides in love abides in God, and God abides in him." 1 John 4:16

May the prayer of your heart today be like David's in Psalm 63:1-3: *"O God, you are my God; earnestly I seek you; my soul thirsts for you; my flesh faints for you, as in a dry and weary land where there is no water. So I have looked upon you in the sanctuary, beholding your power and glory. Because your steadfast love is better than life, my lips will praise you."* Just as David looked upon the Lord in his sanctuary, you can see God daily. Just as he beheld God's power, glory, and love, you can experience God. May you be renewed today as you step out into the world, and may God's strength be your source as you seek to live in light of his glorious nearness.

Extended Reading: 2 Corinthians 4

The Renewal of Your Mind

DAY 16

SCRIPTURE

"Do not be conformed to this world, but be transformed by the renewal of your mind, that by testing you may discern what is the will of God, what is good and acceptable and perfect." Romans 12:2

DEVOTIONAL

The mind is the vehicle in which thoughts and ideas become emotions, beliefs, and actions. You hear things every day that attempt to influence the way you see yourself and your life. Advertising tells you that you are constantly in need of something bigger and better to be happy. People tell you who you are and what you should do based only on their limited perspectives. You also have a very real enemy who hates you, working to convince you that you aren't worth love, you're good at nothing, and you'll never amount to anything. But God, because of his incredible love for you, has given you the Holy Spirit and his word. He's given you the ability to renew your mind to the truth of how he sees you and feels about you, the truth of who you really are. Every day, you have the chance to experience the much needed renewal of your emotions, perspectives, and beliefs. Every day, God longs to speak the truth of your identity through his word and Spirit. So, let's look today at the power of renewing our minds and how we can consistently experience that renewal.

Romans 12:1-2 says, *"I appeal to you therefore, brothers, by the mercies of God, to present your bodies as a living sacrifice, holy and acceptable to God, which is your spiritual worship. Do not be conformed to this world, but be transformed by the renewal of your mind, that by testing you may discern what is the will of God, what is good and acceptable and perfect."* When we renew our minds we are presenting ourselves as worship to God. You worship God when you choose to believe his word over others' words. You love God when you trust him over your feelings and limited perspective. And when you renew your mind, you are conforming no longer to the world, with its destruction and many lies. God puts conforming to the lies of the world and renewing your mind to the truth in stark contrast.

Romans 8:5-6 further illustrates the point: *"Those who live according to the flesh set their minds on the things of the flesh, but those who live according to the Spirit set their minds on the things of the Spirit. For to set the mind on the flesh is death, but to set the mind on the Spirit is life and peace."* When you set your mind on the Spirit, you will begin to experience life in your thoughts. Your way of thinking will be transformed from being negative and destructive to positive and responsive to God's boundless love and grace. What you choose to trust and believe will impact every area of your life for either good or bad.

So in light of the incredible promises of God's word, how can you experience the fruit of renewing your mind? How can you continually set your mind on the things of the Spirit? First, you have to make time to open your mind and heart to Scripture every day. The best time to experience renewal in your mind is when you first wake up. Every morning, you can lay the foundation for what you will believe and how you will think for the rest of the day.

Second, you have to read Scripture while listening to the Holy Spirit. Scripture will come alive when you spend time reading it with the guidance and teaching of the Spirit. In John 14:16-17 Jesus says, *"I will ask the Father, and he will give you another Helper, to be with you forever, even the Spirit of truth, whom the world cannot receive, because it neither sees him nor knows him. You know him, for he dwells with you and will be in you."* Spend time allowing your Helper, the Spirit of truth, to reveal the ways in which he desires to apply Scripture to your life. Ask the Holy Spirit to be your Teacher as your read.

Third, you have to live in obedience to God's word. The Bible isn't merely historical, but a book full of practical and applicable truth that has the ability to change your life. When you open your heart to God's word and choose to believe it, you will experience transformation. When you obey God's commands, they will bear incredible fruit in your life. God's word is meant to direct you to the abundant life he has planned for you. Have faith in the words of Scripture. Choose to believe God's promises.

Last, you must see yourself in light of God's word. You have the choice to believe God or not. The Bible says incredible things about your identity in Christ: *"For our sake he made him to be sin who knew no sin, so that in him we might become the righteousness of God"* (2 Corinthians 5:21). The Bible says that you are God's child, that you are worth the death of Christ and that you are free from the bondage of sin and the world. Those are powerful promises. But in order for you to experience the fullness of what Scripture says, you must renew your way of thinking to be like God's. Paul says that *"we have the mind of Christ"* as people born of the Spirit (1 Corinthians 2:16). So set your mind every day on the things of God. Read Scripture with the help of the Spirit, walk in obedience to God's word, and see yourself as God does. If you will do these things daily, your entire outlook on life will be one of contentment, joy, purpose, and abundance.

Where do you need to renew your mind today? What area of your life seems to be plagued by negativity, insecurity, or anger? Spend time reading God's word with the Holy Spirit. Receive revelation from the very God who authored the word you're reading. Meditate on the words that stand out to you, and allow them to change the way you think, feel, and act. Experience renewal today in your way of thinking, and watch as renewing your mind changes your entire day for the better.

GUIDED PRAYER

1. Meditate on the power of renewing your mind.

"Do not be conformed to this world, but be transformed by the renewal of your mind, that by testing you may discern what is the will of God, what is good and acceptable and perfect." Romans 12:2

"If then you have been raised with Christ, seek the things that are above, where Christ is, seated at the right hand of God. Set your minds on things that are above, not on things that are on earth. For you have died, and your life is hidden with Christ in God." Colossians 3:1-3

2. Reflect on your own life. Where do you need renewal today? What thoughts seem to plague you? Where do you normally feel negative, insecure, or angry?

3. Meditate on a passage of Scripture that seems pertinent to an area of your thinking that needs renewal. Do a web search on a specific topic if you need to. If you're struggling with a particular sin, meditate on Scripture about freedom. If you struggle with your speech, meditate on a passage about taming the tongue. Wherever you need renewal today, God has a plan to help you.

"For those who live according to the flesh set their minds on the things of the flesh, but those who live according to the Spirit set their minds on the things of the Spirit. For to set the mind on the flesh is death, but to set the mind on the Spirit is life and peace." Romans 8:5-6

"Put on the new self, which is being renewed in knowledge after the image of its creator." Colossians 3:10

How great is the love of God that he would give us the incredible gift of his word to mold and shape us! Your heavenly Father loves you too much to let you stay where you are. Every day he has a plan to lead you into more and more abundant life. When you wake up, take a minute to ask yourself what you want your day to be like. What sort of life do you want to live today? Then ask the Spirit to help you renew your mind to God's truth so you can live that life. Walk in freedom today. Live with your mind set on the Spirit. And experience the incredible life God has planned for you as his child. You'll never have a better day than one where your mind is renewed to the truth of God's unfathomable love.

Extended Reading: Romans 12

Renewal of Your First Love

DAY 17

DEVOTIONAL

Out of God's great desire to be truly loved by his people, we have been given the gift of free will to choose who and what we will give our affections to. God, knowing full well that not all of us would choose to love him, still created us out of his longing for close relationship with us. You see, so great is our heavenly Father's desire for relationship with us that he suffers as he watches his children choose to love people, ideas, and possessions that will never fully love us in return. So great is his love for us that he responds to our sin of idolatry with grace and mercy every single time. And so vast is his affection for us that he sent his only Son so that we might be restored to close relationship with our heavenly Father once again. But still, we choose to love things other than God. Still we seek out satisfaction and love from creation rather than the Creator. Still we choose to place our hope and affections in the world instead of in God. If we are to live the life God intends for us, the only fulfilling life possible, we need a renewal of our first love.

Thousands of years ago, the church in Ephesus was much like we are today. Revelation 2:4 says in reference to the church in Ephesus, *"But I have this against you, that you have abandoned the love you had at first."* The Ephesians were still working and waiting for God. They hadn't abandoned their faith, just their first love. But Scripture makes it clear that when it comes down to it in the end, what will be most important is the way in which we have loved God. When asked what the most important commandment was, Jesus replied, *"You shall love the Lord your God with all your heart and with all your soul and with all your strength and with all your mind"* (Luke 10:27). Loving God is our first priority. Our love for God is the foundation on which all of life is to be lived. 1 Corinthians 13:1-3 says, *"If I speak in the tongues of men and of angels, but have not love, I am a noisy gong or a clanging cymbal. And if I have prophetic powers, and understand all mysteries and all knowledge, and if I have all faith, so as to remove mountains, but have not love, I am nothing. If I give away all I have, and if I deliver up my body to be burned, but have not love, I gain nothing."* This life is all about the posture of your heart.

> *"But I have this against you, that you have abandoned the love you had at first."*
>
> **REVELATION 2:4**

Reflect for a minute on just how incredible the love of our God is. Scripture makes it clear that he isn't after our service first, but our love. He only desires us to work with him if it is done out of our love for him. If we prophesy, show incredible acts of faith, or even give up our lives for him out of anything but love, he calls it *"a noisy gong or a clanging cymbal."* God is after your heart. More than anything else in the world, he wants to love you and be loved by you. Of course he wants you to co-labor with him and obey his commandments, but only out of love for him. Yes, he wants you to lead others to him, but out of the desire to share the incredible love you've been shown. Too often we size up our relationship with God based on how often we've gone to church, how many mission trips we've been on, how many people we've won to Jesus, how many committees we've served on, or how much of our finances we've given to God. And too often we do all of that trying to win over a God who already loves us more than we could ever ask or imagine. God is the father in the prodigal son story running out to meet you and celebrate you regardless of anything you've ever done or will do. He's the shepherd who leaves the ninety-nine to go after the one. He's the God who leaves his throne to die for the very people who shouted, "Crucify him, crucify him!" And he's the God who waits patiently every day to show you the depth of his love, that nothing you could ever do will change the way he loves you.

Nothing could be more important than living your life on the foundation of God's greatest commandment: to love him. And while it's incredibly important to spend your life loving God, he knows you will only be able to do so if you've encountered his love first. 1 John 4:19 says, *"We love because he first loved us."* Experiencing God's love is the beginning and end to everything we do as his children. It's out of encountering the affections of our heavenly Father that our hearts will be stirred to love him back. Let's take time today to encounter the love of our heavenly Father and let his kindness draw us to repentance (Romans 2:4). Encounter the heart of God, and let his love renew within you your first love.

GUIDED PRAYER

1. Meditate on God's love for you as revealed in his word. Receive his presence. Let him speak his love straight to your heart.

"But God shows his love for us in that while we were still sinners, Christ died for us." Romans 5:8

"Who shall separate us from the love of Christ? Shall tribulation, or distress, or persecution, or famine, or nakedness, or danger, or sword? As it is written, 'For your sake we are being killed all the day long; we are regarded as sheep to be slaughtered.' No, in all these things we are more than conquerors through him who loved us. For I am sure that neither death nor life, nor angels nor rulers, nor things present nor things to come, nor powers, nor height nor depth, nor anything else in all creation, will be able to separate us from the love of God in Christ Jesus our Lord." Romans 8:35-39

2. Reflect on your own life. Where do you seem to chase after the affections of the world before God? What idols are in your own heart? Who or what do you love more than God?

"But I have this against you, that you have abandoned the love you had at first." Revelation 2:4

3. Ask the Lord to heal those places of your heart. Be drawn to repentance from God's kindness. Repent to him the places where you've idolized someone or something. Receive the healing that happens when you confess your sins.

"If we confess our sins, he is faithful and just to forgive us our sins and to cleanse us from all unrighteousness." 1 John 1:9

The Bible is clear that God will always forgive our sins as believers. His heart is always for restoration. He always desires to lead us to a life where our hearts are in no way veiled before him. Idols and sin tie us down to the world in ways that keep us from the fullness of relationship available in God. Engage in the act of confession. Spend time consistently giving your sin over to God, and receive the healing and renewal he longs to bring you. May your day be filled with peace as the result of God's forgiveness, nearness, and loving-kindness.

Extended Reading: 1 Corinthians 13

Renewal of Joy

DAY 18

DEVOTIONAL

When I think of the word "joy" I often picture the unadulterated smile of a child's face. Children have this ability to have joy simply because they've found the delight of their parents. The joy of a child is unlike anything most of us experience as we grow up. For most of us, true joy has been crowded out by the pressures and cares of responsibility. Joy becomes contingent upon the circumstances of our lives. Most of us feel the pressure of finances, work, relationships, and even serving God consistently to the point that joy is a pursuit we've almost given up on. But God has a message and a plan for you for a renewal of consistent and unshakable joy. Let's open our hearts and minds to dive into everything God has in store for us as we spend time encountering his desire to bring us joy.

Our joy is not to be of this world, but of God. Psalm 16:11 says, *"You make known to me the path of life; in your presence there is fullness of joy; at your right hand are pleasures forevermore."* The fullness of joy will only be found in God's presence, and the Bible tells us that God's presence is everywhere! Psalm 139:7-10 says, *"Where shall I go from your Spirit? Or where shall I flee from your presence? If I ascend to heaven, you are there! If I make my bed in Sheol, you are there! If I take the wings*

*"Restore to me the joy of your salvation,
and uphold me with a willing spirit."*

PSALM 51:12

of the morning and dwell in the uttermost parts of the sea, even there your hand shall lead me, and your right hand shall hold me." Because God is everywhere and in his presence is fullness of joy, joy is available to you 24/7. And Scripture teaches us in Romans 14:17 that *"The kingdom of God is not a matter of eating and drinking but of righteousness and peace and joy in the Holy Spirit."* God's lordship in our lives is all about *"righteousness and peace and joy."* Our heavenly Father desires to bring about those incredible fruits of the Spirit in you today. He has a plan to lead you to perfect, unshakable joy. But in order to receive the incredible gift your God wants to give you today, you will have to make a choice to place your hope and trust in him.

Scripture tells us that our joy is to be wholeheartedly found in God and not in the world. The joy our heavenly Father longs to bring us is meant to transcend anything this world could ever do to us. But in order for God's desire to come to fruition in our lives, we have to place our hope and trust solely in him. Psalm 33:21 says, *"Our heart is glad in him, because we trust in his holy name."* Romans 15:13 says, *"May the God of hope fill you with all joy and peace in believing, so that by the power of the Holy Spirit you may abound in hope."* What we place our trust and belief in becomes the rudder that guides our emotions. If you place your trust in your job, people, or finances, you are building a foundation for your joy that can be crushed at a moment's notice. But if you will choose today to place your trust and hope in your Lord Jesus Christ, you will have a sure foundation unshakable by any trial or circumstance that comes your way. In fact, those very trials that had the power to destroy your joy will, in God, become yet another source of it.

James 1:2-4 says, *"Count it all joy, my brothers, when you meet trials of various kinds, for you know that the testing of your faith produces steadfastness. And let steadfastness have its full effect, that you may be perfect and complete, lacking in nothing."* When you place your hope and trust in God, your eyes will be opened to see the incredible work he is doing in you through any and every circumstance. Whether you have success in this life or not, you will have joy because your life will be wholly lived with your relationship with God as first priority. When your goal is to see God's kingdom come to earth, the circumstances of your job and relationships won't have the power to shake your joy and satisfaction any longer. You see, God's plan to is to redeem your life totally and completely. God's plan is to renew your joy every morning as you place your hope and trust in him alone.

Spend time today with your heavenly Father doing that very thing. Reflect on your life and see what has had the ability to shake your joy. May your joy become like that of a child's today, who simply delights in the love of the Father. *"May you be strengthened with all power, according to his glorious might, for all endurance and patience with joy."* Colossians 1:11

GUIDED PRAYER

1. Meditate on the joy God has in store for those who place their trust in him.

"For our heart is glad in him, because we trust in his holy name." Psalm 33:21

"You make known to me the path of life; in your presence there is fullness of joy; at your right hand are pleasures forevermore." Psalm 16:11

2. Reflect on your own life. What has the power to steal your joy? Where have you been placing your trust and hope?

3. Place your hope and trust in your heavenly Father today. Choose to give him your heart instead of the world. Make your relationship with him first priority.

"A joyful heart is good medicine, but a crushed spirit dries up the bones." Proverbs 17:22

How incredible is the heart of our God that he would consistently and constantly bring us joy! Your God has such a love for you that he never wants you to go a day without it. He never wants you to have a moment without his unshakable joy. Jesus said in John 10:10, *"The thief comes only to steal and kill and destroy. I came that they may have life and have it abundantly."* Experience the abundant life your God has in store for you as you live your life in a wholehearted pursuit of the joy of your good and present heavenly Father.

Extended Reading: Psalm 139

Renewal of Purpose

DAY 19

DEVOTIONAL

You and I were born with a deep desire to live with purpose. As children, we dream of doing something significant with our lives. We dream of being a person who makes a difference in the world. Inherent in all of us is a longing to make a deep and lasting impact. Our longing for purpose only becomes a problem as we begin seeking out its source. Most of us live our lives in constant pursuit of finding out why we're here, seeking the answer to the question: "What am I uniquely made for?" And we look for the answers in all the wrong places. We look for our purpose in each other, in the ever-changing whims of society, or internally, in what seems to make us feel good in the moment. But God has a better purpose for our lives than we could ever find in the world. He has a purpose so great, so powerful, and so lasting that when we get a glimpse of it, we will forever be changed. God has a page in his grand narrative written just for you, to use you to make a unique and eternal impact on the earth.

Jeremiah 29:11 says, *"For I know the plans I have for you, declares the Lord, plans for welfare and not for evil, to give you a future and a hope."* Let us not miss the importance of what God would reveal to us today because we've heard something before. Instead, let's dive in deeper and see what God's word would reveal to us about that purpose. In John 15:16 Jesus says, *"You did not choose me, but I chose you and appointed you that you should go and bear fruit and that your fruit should abide."* You are chosen by God. You aren't secondary to someone else in God's kingdom. He has formed you and chosen you to *"go and bear fruit."* And Jesus desires that our fruit would *"abide."* He has chosen you to make a lasting impact on the earth.

So, what lasting fruit does God intend for you here? Answering this question should start with the words of Jesus. Allow God's commandments to lay the defining foundation of your purpose. In response to the question of what the greatest commandment is, Jesus replies, *"And you shall love the Lord your God with all your heart and with all your soul and with all your mind and with all your strength.' The second is this: 'You shall love your neighbor as yourself.' There is no other commandment greater than these"* (Mark 12:30-31). Your purpose here on earth is to love God and

> *"You did not choose me, but I chose you and appointed you that you should go and bear fruit and that your fruit should abide."*
>
> **JOHN 15:16**

love others. God has chosen to use love to bring about salvation. He's chosen to use love as the catalyst for spiritual awakening. It's love that is God's driving force, and it's love that he longs to instill in us as our highest goal. Understand today that you are formed and called to love above all else.

Scripture also tells us that we have been chosen to be carriers and ministers of the kingdom of God. Jesus said in Mark 1:15, *"The time is fulfilled, and the kingdom of God is at hand; repent and believe in the gospel."* God's kingdom is here on earth. And Revelation 5:10 says, *"You have made them a kingdom and priests to our God, and they shall reign on the earth."* We are not purposed to merely suffer and wait for heaven. God's kingdom is here on earth, and we are his workmanship. We are his priests. Acts 26:16 says, *"Rise and stand upon your feet, for I have appeared to you for this purpose, to appoint you as a servant and witness to the things in which you have seen me and to those in which I will appear to you."* Matthew 28:19 says, *"Go therefore and make disciples of all nations, baptizing them in the name of the Father and of the Son and of the Holy Spirit."*

Your life here is of eternal value. A life spent simply waiting for heaven is a life wasted. God has placed an eternal purpose on your life, a purpose meant to be pursued and lived out every minute of every day. You don't have time to waste. And the compelling truth is, you will never be satisfied until you devote your life to ministering this incredible gospel of restoration and love. Until you pursue seeing God's kingdom come through your job, relationships, and time, you will never experience the joy and passion only God's purpose can bring you. God doesn't have a cookie-cutter mold he tries to fit all believers into. He's formed you for a specific and unique purpose no other believer will be able to accomplish. His plans for you are your own and no other's. So choose today to live your life for your heavenly Father. Work with him in all that you do. Love him and others with every fiber of your being. And experience the joy of making a deep, eternal impact with all that you do. May God renew your sense of purpose today as you enter into a time of guided prayer.

GUIDED PRAYER

1. Meditate on God's desire to use you for an incredible purpose.

"And you have made them a kingdom and priests to our God, and they shall reign on the earth." Revelation 5:10

"But you are a chosen race, a royal priesthood, a holy nation, a people for his own possession, that you may proclaim the excellencies of him who called you out of darkness into his marvelous light." 1 Peter 2:9

"You did not choose me, but I chose you and appointed you that you should go and bear fruit and that your fruit should abide." John 15:16

2. Reflect on your own life for a moment. In what ways have you been living out of a purpose other than God's? Confess those sins to your loving heavenly Father. Let his forgiveness transform your heart.

3. Now commit your life to God's plan and purpose. Choose to love with all you have today. Line up your heart with God's word, and pursue the life he has in store for you. Give him your job, your family, and finances. Ask him how he would have you use them.

"Or do you not know that your body is a temple of the Holy Spirit within you, whom you have from God? You are not your own, for you were bought with a price. So glorify God in your body." 1 Corinthians 6:19-20

"But rise and stand upon your feet, for I have appeared to you for this purpose, to appoint you as a servant and witness to the things in which you have seen me and to those in which I will appear to you." Acts 26:16

What will God say about your life when you get finished here? Will your life have been spent in pursuit of him and his kingdom or in building up a small kingdom here that will pass away like the changing of seasons? Will your life be of fleeting or eternal impact? Only you can choose how you will live your life. May you make the choice today and every day to live the only life that truly matters. God has incredible plans and purposes in store for you if you will simply open your heart and your hands to him and say, "Use me."

Extended Reading: John 10:1-19

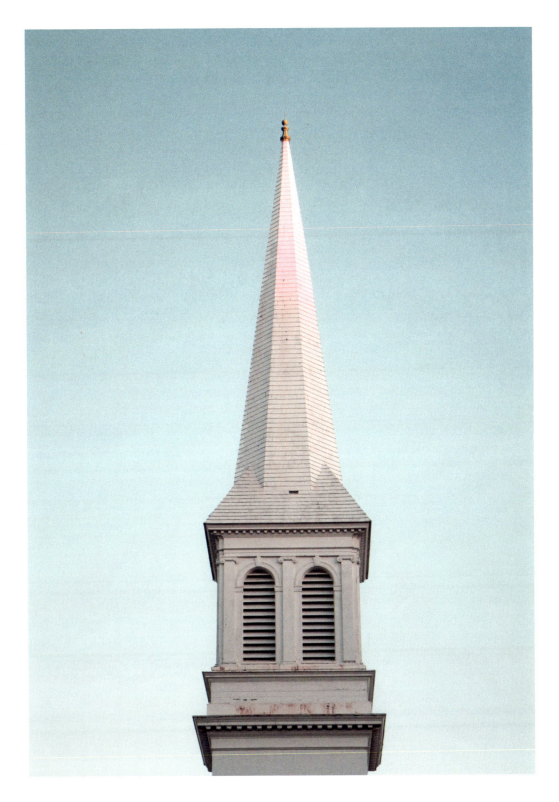

Renewal of Conscience

DAY 20

DEVOTIONAL

Our conscience is a window revealing how we view ourselves and, most importantly, our relationship with God. One of the worst effects sin has is distorting our view of ourselves in relation to God. The devil's plan with sin was always to separate us from God, so Jesus came to the earth to destroy the power of sin in our lives. He came so that we might have restored relationship with our heavenly Father. But still sin persists. Even though the power of sin was broken, its effects destroyed, we often still live with an unclean conscience. We feel that God is angry with us, that he doesn't want to be with us, or that we can't come before him and sit at his feet. Your conscience affects your relationship with God either negatively or positively. It will either lead you to God's throne room or away from his presence. Your heavenly Father's desire today is that you would come to see yourself as he does, that your conscience would be wiped clean, and that sin and lies would separate you from him no longer.

Hebrews 10:19-23 contains an important truth for us today. Scripture says:

Therefore, brothers, since we have confidence to enter the holy places by the blood of Jesus, by the new and living way that he opened for us through the curtain, that is, through his flesh, and since we have a great priest over the house of God, let us draw near with a true heart in full assurance of faith, with our hearts sprinkled clean from an evil conscience and our bodies washed with pure water. Let us hold fast the confession of our hope without wavering, for he who promised is faithful.

Let the truth of Scripture sink into your heart. Hebrews tells us that our confidence to come before God is found in the blood of Jesus. Through his death, Jesus paved the way for you to come before the throne of God with confidence and full assurance of faith. God's desire today is that your conscience would be *"sprinkled clean"* with the powerful blood of your Savior.

So, let's dive even deeper into how God sees us today. Let the truth of his word further mold your identity until it is perfectly aligned with his perspective. Galatians 3:26-28 says, *"For in Christ Jesus you are all sons of God, through faith. For as many of you as were baptized into Christ have put on Christ. There is neither*

> *"Let us draw near with a true heart in full assurance of faith, with our hearts sprinkled clean from an evil conscience and our bodies washed with pure water."*
>
> HEBREWS 10:22

Jew nor Greek, there is neither slave nor free, there is no male and female, for you are all one in Christ Jesus." 1 John 1:9 says, *"If we confess our sins, he is faithful and just to forgive us our sins and to cleanse us from all unrighteousness."* Romans 8:1 says, *"There is therefore now no condemnation for those who are in Christ Jesus."* Philippians 3:20 says, *"But our citizenship is in heaven, and from it we await a Savior, the Lord Jesus Christ."* 1 Thessalonians 5:5 says, *"For you are all children of light, children of the day. We are not of the night or of the darkness."* 1 Peter 2:9 says, *"But you are a chosen race, a royal priesthood, a holy nation, a people for his own possession, that you may proclaim the excellencies of him who called you out of darkness into his marvelous light."* And Colossians 1:21-22 says, *"And you, who once were alienated and hostile in mind, doing evil deeds, he has now reconciled in his body of flesh by his death, in order to present you holy and blameless and above reproach before him."*

Your heavenly Father sees you as he sees Jesus. Many Christians believe that while they are clothed with Christ, they're still dirty and sinful on the inside. But don't be deceived today. At salvation you were made completely new. 2 Corinthians 5:17 says, *"Therefore, if anyone is in Christ, he is a new creation."* God didn't trick himself with the death of Jesus. He sees you completely. And when he looks at you, he sees the blood of Jesus running through your veins. He sees you as his clean and holy child. Through the death of Jesus, you can see God with unveiled face. 2 Corinthians 3:16-18 says, *"But when one turns to the Lord, the veil is removed. Now the Lord is the Spirit, and where the Spirit of the Lord is, there is freedom. And we all, with unveiled face, beholding the glory of the Lord, are being transformed into the same image from one degree of glory to another. For this comes from the Lord who is the Spirit."* You can see and know God freely and fully. In fact, that's God's greatest desire. He longs for us to know him. He longs for us to encounter the depth of his love and affections for us every day.

Sit at the feet of your loving heavenly Father with the knowledge that there is nothing in the way of you and him. Spend time with him allowing the truth of how he sees you to renew your conscience. May your conscience, renewed in him, lead you freely and consistently to the throne of God.

GUIDED PRAYER

1. Meditate on your new identity in Christ.

"For you are all children of light, children of the day. We are not of the night or of the darkness." 1 Thessalonians 5:5

"But our citizenship is in heaven, and from it we await a Savior, the Lord Jesus Christ." Philippians 3:20

"There is therefore now no condemnation for those who are in Christ Jesus." Romans 8:1

"Therefore, if anyone is in Christ, he is a new creation." 2 Corinthians 5:17

2. Reflect on your own conscience. How do you view yourself? Through what lens do you see your relationship with God? Is it one renewed by the blood of Jesus or one inconsistent with his word?

3. Allow God's truth to clean your conscience today. Come before God boldly, and let him do a work in how you view your identity.

"Therefore, brothers, since we have confidence to enter the holy places by the blood of Jesus, by the new and living way that he opened for us through the curtain, that is, through his flesh, and since we have a great priest over the house of God, let us draw near with a true heart in full assurance of faith, with our hearts sprinkled clean from an evil conscience and our bodies washed with pure water. Let us hold fast the confession of our hope without wavering, for he who promised is faithful." Hebrews 10:19-23

Whenever you feel like something is in the way of you and God, take a minute to reflect on your conscience. Ask yourself, "Do I feel worthy to be with God? Is something leading me away from him instead of to him?" Ask the Spirit to renew your conscience in that moment. Spend a minute gaining God's perspective. Confess whatever sin you committed to God, and allow his forgiveness to draw you near. Nothing could be more important than spending time with your heavenly Father with a clean conscience that you might experience the fullness of his affection for you.

Extended Reading: 1 Peter 2:1-12

Renewal of Perspective

DAY 21

DEVOTIONAL

This life is like a gust of wind, strong and tangible, but as fleeting as it is real. Tragically, most of us spend the majority of our lives just trying to find out why we're here. We ask, "What's our purpose? What's the point of all this? What's the meaning of life?" While Scripture is clear that this life is fleeting, God also makes it abundantly clear that what we do with our lives here is of eternal significance. We have incredibly important things to do and little time to do them. So, to truly live life to the fullest as God desires for us, to make the impact we alone can make in this life, we need a clear understanding of how fleeting and important our lives are. We need a renewal of perspective.

1 John 2:17 says, *"The world is passing away along with its desires, but whoever does the will of God abides forever."* God has a plan for you and a will for your life. Your abilities, mind, heart, and hands are of incredible importance to him. Ephesians 2:10 says, *"For we are his workmanship, created in Christ Jesus for good works, which God prepared beforehand, that we should walk in them."* Your heavenly Father has works prepared for you that only you can accomplish. He has plans for you that he does not have for anybody else. But he has also given you the ability to lead your own life. Every day you have the choice to surrender your life to the lordship of Jesus and follow the guidance of his Spirit. Or, you can choose to go

"And the world is passing away along with its desires, but whoever does the will of God abides forever."

1 JOHN 2:17

through life being your own boss, making decisions and plans on your own without his guidance. Only one choice will lead you to a life spent co-laboring with God and making an eternal impact. Only one choice will lead you to the joy and purpose you were created for. Only one choice will assure you at the end of your days that you made a deep and lasting impact with your life.

You see, there isn't enough time to waste any part of your life pursuing the things of the world. There aren't enough days to spend even a single one building your kingdom instead of God's. And your life will be measured by the way in which you loved God and others, not by the weight of your possessions, accolades, or status. Jesus commands us in Matthew 6:19-21, *"Do not lay up for yourselves treasures on earth, where moth and rust destroy and where thieves break in and steal, but lay up for yourselves treasures in heaven, where neither moth nor rust destroys and where thieves do not break in and steal. For where your treasure is, there your heart will be also."* Jesus illustrates an often missed point here: the value of your life is your heart. God is the Creator of all treasure, of everything beautiful, but his prized possession is your heart. His deepest longing is for your affections. He knows that when you give your heart to the world, to pursuing earthly objectives, you will miss out on the peace and purpose of living your life with a constant eternal perspective. Scripture tells us that though we are here on earth, this is not our home. We are called to live here with urgency, maintaining a renewed perspective of our time. Paul writes in Ephesians 5:15-17, *"Look carefully then how you walk, not as unwise but as wise, making the best use of the time, because the days are evil. Therefore do not be foolish, but understand what the will of the Lord is."* Will you live your life in light of God's will for you or your own? Will you surrender your heart to the Lord every day or keep one foot in the world and one foot in the kingdom of God?

The choice is entirely up to you. You have both the Holy Spirit and the world vying for your heart. But only God will reward your affections with his own. Only God gave up his life entirely out of his unending devotion and love for you. All you have to do to live fully for God is encounter the love of your heavenly Father each day and live in response to that love by loving him and others. When you are faithful to listen, God is faithful to guide you day to day and season to season. His kingship demands our obedience, and his love stirs our hearts until obedience to him is natural. Experience both the majesty and love of your King today. Let the Holy Spirit lead you to a life of radical, loving obedience. Allow the Spirit and the word to renew your perspective on the purpose of your life. And choose today to live with eternal perspective by loving your heavenly Father and others.

GUIDED PRAYER

1. Meditate on both the fleeting nature and importance of this life.

"Remember how short my time is! For what vanity you have created all the children of man! What man can live and never see death? Who can deliver his soul from the power of Sheol?" Psalm 89:47-48

"For we are his workmanship, created in Christ Jesus for good works, which God prepared beforehand, that we should walk in them." Ephesians 2:10

2. Reflect on your own life. In what areas have you been pursuing the world instead of God? Where have you chosen to rule your own life? What decisions have you made apart from the leadership of God? Confess those sins to the Lord, and receive his forgiveness. He longs to restore you totally to himself. He will daily forgive your sins and lead you fully to the life he has in store for you.

3. Commit yourself to live for the kingdom of God instead of your own. Pray to the Lord, and tell him your desire to live for his kingdom. Submit your will and live for him instead of yourself. Ask for the help of the Spirit as you go through your day. Listen for his voice and follow his leading as you pray.

This life requires a daily process of confession, forgiveness, and commitment. Daily we need to gain fresh perspective on what really matters. Constantly throughout our day we need to remind ourselves of why we were created. Engage in this process, encounter the grace of God as you make mistakes, and live your life pursuing all that God has in store for you. You can never experience the same peace, purpose, and grace-filled love anywhere else as you will living fully surrendered to God. God will never forsake you or reject you. He has only love for you. Choose him over the world today and experience the life you've been longing for.

Extended Reading: Matthew 6

DAYS 22 - 28

Transformation

04

WEEK

"And we all, with unveiled face, beholding the glory of the Lord, are being transformed into the same image from one degree of glory to another." 2 Corinthians 3:8

WEEKLY OVERVIEW

We serve a God of powerful transformations. All throughout Scripture God takes those whom the world deemed the lowest, the hopeless, and the helpless and uses them to change the world. You are not beyond transformation. God longs to break off that which inhibits you from experiencing fullness of life. He longs to heal you, deliver you, and set you free. May your life be forever changed as we spend time discovering God's heart for transformation.

Seeking Transformation

DAY 22

DEVOTIONAL

As humans burdened and suffering from both our sins and the fallen nature of the world around us, we are in desperate need of transformation. We are in desperate need of help from a God who has the power to not just clean us up on the outside but to transform us at the core of who we are. But this God doesn't force transformation on us. He works when we make space for him to do so. If we're going to experience the freedom, joy, and purpose that can only come from the inner working of the Holy Spirit, we must be those who seek transformation.

> *"Create in me a clean heart, O God,
> and renew a right spirit within me."*
>
> **PSALM 51:10**

Psalm 51:10-12 says, *"Create in me a clean heart, O God, and renew a right spirit within me. Cast me not away from your presence, and take not your Holy Spirit from me. Restore to me the joy of your salvation, and uphold me with a willing spirit."* Here in Psalm 51 David exemplifies the heart of one who seeks transformation. He models for us a posture of humility that will lead to powerful encounters with God's transformative love. He doesn't sit back and merely live with that which plagues him but goes to God with his problems that he might be changed.

David begins as we all should in asking for God to do a mighty work in his heart. And in this act of asking God to create in him a clean heart, David opens himself up to receive the powerful work of the Holy Spirit. To receive transformation from God we have to come before him humbly and honestly that he might have space to do the impossible in our lives.

Often we spend a majority of our efforts trying to convince others and ourselves that we don't need help. We work tirelessly to build up a facade that we have it all together. We do everything we can to maintain a sense of control in our lives—even in regard to our spirituality. But in doing so we place appearances above reality. We allow that which is destroying us from the inside to persist simply because we are unwilling to acknowledge that we have need. It's as if we tried to cover up an external wound with jewelry expecting the surface-level beauty of something to contain the power to heal what's underneath. We don't need that which covers up. We need the healing that comes from going with an honest, open heart to the one true Healer.

God's heart for you and me today is that we would put down our guards, take an honest look at our hearts, and recognize our need for transformation. He longs for us to take a moment and call out that which is robbing us of the abundant life he so willingly died to give us. Your God is willing and able to transform you. That which has plagued you for so long will be healed and broken off your life if you will continually seek transformation from your loving heavenly Father. May you experience powerful transformation today as you enter into a time of guided prayer.

GUIDED PRAYER

1. Meditate on the importance of seeking transformation. Allow Psalm 51:10-12 to be your model.

"Create in me a clean heart, O God, and renew a right spirit within me. Cast me not away from your presence, and take not your Holy Spirit from me. Restore to me the joy of your salvation, and uphold me with a willing spirit." Psalm 51:10-12

2. Take an honest look at your heart. Where do you need transformation? What lie, habitual sin, perspective, or fear is robbing you of abundant life? What's chaining you to the ways, cares, and burdens of the world?

3. Declare your need for transformation in that area to God. Tell him you need his help. Ask him to come and do a mighty work in your heart. Listen to whatever he would speak over you, and trust that he will transform you if you continually seek his help.

"If we confess our sins, he is faithful and just to forgive us our sins and to cleanse us from all unrighteousness." 1 John 1:9

We all have areas in which we need transformation. We all are in need of God's help. Not one of us is perfect. Rather than spending all your energy trying to keep up appearances with others, yourself, and with God, devote yourself completely to living honestly and humbly. Stop exhausting yourself doing that which is of no value and seek help. If you will commit to seeking continual transformation, your efforts will produce life and peace rather than more burden. May your heart be filled with hope as the Holy Spirit works in your life today.

Extended Reading: Psalm 51

God Transforms Us Into New Creations

DAY 23

DEVOTIONAL

One of the greatest lies told to those who have been redeemed by the blood of Jesus relates to our old and new natures. So many believers live under the oppression of the lie that God in his grace may see us as clean, but at our core we're truly not. We live as if redemption in Jesus is like clean clothes covering up the dirt and filth that will always remain, and as if redemption is our get-to-heaven-free card. We hold fast to a belief that salvation was more of an illusion of redemption than an actual transformation. And those lies act like weights dragging us back to the ways and sins of our former selves.

> *"Therefore, if anyone is in Christ, he is a new creation. The old has passed away; behold, the new has come."*
>
> **2 CORINTHIANS 5:17**

Scripture could not speak more clearly of the opposite. 2 Corinthians 5:17-21 says:

Therefore, if anyone is in Christ, he is a new creation. The old has passed away; behold, the new has come. All this is from God, who through Christ reconciled us to himself and gave us the ministry of reconciliation; that is, in Christ God was reconciling the world to himself, not counting their trespasses against them, and entrusting to us the message of reconciliation. Therefore, we are ambassadors for Christ, God making his appeal through us. We implore you on behalf of Christ, be reconciled to God. For our sake he made him to be sin who knew no sin, so that in him we might become the righteousness of God.

If you are in Christ today—if you are saved—then you are a new creation. The old hasn't stuck around until you die; *"The old has passed away; behold, the new has come."* You see, the fact that you have been transformed into a new creation doesn't have anything to do with your sins, failures, and beliefs. Transformation in Jesus is based on his power, not yours. Truth is based on his sacrifice, not your actions. You are a new creation totally and completely by the grace of God, apart from any of your works—as righteous or sinful as they may be. *"For our sake he made him to be sin who knew no sin, so that in him we might become the righteousness of God."*

Don't live today with your experience as your truth. Don't see yourself based on your works but rather on the truth of what Scripture says about you. If you will begin to believe that God truly has already transformed you into a new creation and reconciled you to himself simply by grace, then you will live and act on a foundation that births freedom and righteousness. But, if you set your mind on the things of the flesh, which is in opposition to the reality of transformation already worked in you at the cross, then you will live chained to the ways of your former self (Romans 8:6).

Take time today to reflect on your new nature in Jesus. Allow Scripture and the Holy Spirit to help you see yourself as one transformed and set free by grace. Commit yourself to live with grace as your source rather than your own strength. And experience freedom today that comes from living with a renewed mind.

GUIDED PRAYER

1. Meditate on your new nature in Christ. Allow Scripture to be your foundation for truth, not your experience.

"Therefore, if anyone is in Christ, he is a new creation. The old has passed away; behold, the new has come." 2 Corinthians 5:17

2. Where does your life not line up with the truth that you are a new creation? What is entangling you to the things of the world? Where are you not experiencing the life of the Spirit?

"For God has done what the law, weakened by the flesh, could not do. By sending his own Son in the likeness of sinful flesh and for sin, he condemned sin in the flesh, in order that the righteous requirement of the law might be fulfilled in us, who walk not according to the flesh but according to the Spirit." Romans 8:3-4

3. Confess any sin to God and ask for his help in living by the Spirit. Ask the Spirit for a revelation of what it looks like to live with him as your source rather than your own strength. Ask him for a heart-level revelation of your new nature.

"I have been crucified with Christ. It is no longer I who live, but Christ who lives in me. And the life I now live in the flesh I live by faith in the Son of God, who loved me and gave himself for me." Galatians 2:20

Foundational to living a life that lines up with truth of who God says you are is living by grace. In our own strength we can accomplish nothing. We have no power over sin in and of ourselves. We have no power to live free from the ways of the world when we try to live based on our works. That's why Romans 8:3 says, *"For God has done what the law, weakened by the flesh, could not do."* He fulfilled the requirement of the law that we might live by grace. He set us free from living in our own strength by filling us with the Holy Spirit, our great Helper. Stop living in your own strength and learn to live by grace. Learn to feel, think, and act on the foundation of grace. Your heavenly Father who loves you has given you all you need to live as a new creation. He has done it all. So take hold of who you are in Jesus and experience a life transformed by the reality of God's power and love.

Extended Reading: Galatians 2

Continual Transformation

DAY 24

DEVOTIONAL

Oftentimes we see transformation as a one-time act. We find a problem and work on it until it gets better, then we go back to living life as normal. But the heart of God is for continual transformation. God longs that we would be so open and aware of the desire of the Spirit that we allow him to transform us every moment of every day.

WEEK 4

> *"I appeal to you therefore, brothers, by the mercies of God, to present your bodies as a living sacrifice, holy and acceptable to God, which is your spiritual worship."*
>
> **ROMANS 12:1**

Too often we just accept that we are who we are as if the God we serve didn't have the power to continually set us free. We live as if the Holy Spirit is a God who only shows up every now and then to shake things up then retreats back into the heavens. But God is both loving and present. He is always there for us. He is always filled with desire for us. And the Holy Spirit is constantly ready to lead us, in love, out of the darkness and into the marvelous light of abundant life.

So what does continual transformation look like? How do we live in sync with the Spirit who can constantly change us from the inside out? Romans 12:1 says, *"I appeal to you therefore, brothers, by the mercies of God, to present your bodies as a living sacrifice, holy and acceptable to God, which is your spiritual worship."* Continual transformation will come when we decide to stop living for ourselves and instead become a living sacrifice to God as our *"holy, acceptable"* act of *"spiritual worship."*

You see, when we live for ourselves we naturally take control of our own lives and therefore subjugate God and his desire to transform us. When our limited perspective on what's good in life guides us rather than the perfect, transcendent perspective of God, we will only receive transformation from God when we desperately need it. But, when we seek to be a living sacrifice to God at all times our hearts become open to all the Spirit is doing, saying, and feeling in every moment. If you want to be continually transformed by the powerful, life-changing love of God, you have to choose every day to center your life around the will and desires of God.

Psalm 139:23-24 says, *"Search me, O God, and know my heart! Try me and know my thoughts! And see if there be any grievous way in me, and lead me in the way everlasting!"* May David's prayer be our prayer today as we enter into a time of guided prayer.

GUIDED PRAYER

1. Meditate on God's heart to continually transform you. Reflect on his nearness and his desire to heal you, deliver you, and empower you.

"The Lord your God is in your midst, a mighty one who will save." Zephaniah 3:17

"Fear not, for I am with you; be not dismayed, for I am your God; I will strengthen you, I will help you, I will uphold you with my righteous right hand." Isaiah 41:10

2. Take a moment to assess your heart. Are you seeking to be a living sacrifice to God in all you do? Or are you living with your own desires and will as the foundation of your life?

3. Decide to be a living sacrifice today. Decide to live with the desires and will of God as your foundation. Center your life around the goodness, nearness, and power of your loving Father.

"I appeal to you therefore, brothers, by the mercies of God, to present your bodies as a living sacrifice, holy and acceptable to God, which is your spiritual worship." Romans 12:1

Choosing to be a living sacrifice is a daily decision. Without spending consistent time in God's presence there is no hope for continual transformation. It's only when we encounter the kindness of God that we are able to respond with surrender. It's only upon meeting with God that we live with his power and love as our foundation. Living sacrificially is not something you do in your own strength. Rather, it is the natural response of those who see God for who he truly is. May you commit yourself to experience the reality of God's presence today. And may your life be an act of worship in response to the great love you've been shown.

Extended Reading: Isaiah 41

WEEK 4

125

Transformation through Experience

DAY 25

DEVOTIONAL

No Christian practice can take the place of experiencing God. It's in experiencing God that we begin to live in response to the unconditional, unfathomable depths of God's love. It's in experiencing God that we learn to discern and trust his perfect, pleasing will. And it's in experiencing God that our hearts are transformed into powerful reflections of his wonderful character.

> *"And we all, with unveiled face, beholding the glory of the Lord, are being transformed into the same image from one degree of glory to another. For this comes from the Lord who is the Spirit."*
>
> **2 CORINTHIANS 3:18**

2 Corinthians 3:18 says, *"And we all, with unveiled face, beholding the glory of the Lord, are being transformed into the same image from one degree of glory to another. For this comes from the Lord who is the Spirit."* When we see God face-to-face everything changes. You can't see God and stay the same. Encountering him always requires something from us. Experiencing his holiness always calls us to be holy as he is holy (1 Peter 1:15). Experiencing his love always calls to love because he has *"first loved us"* (1 John 4:19). And experiencing his heart for transformation always calls us to surrender our lives to him as a *"living sacrifice, holy and pleasing"* (Romans 12:1).

In Isaiah 6:1-6, Isaiah's encounter with the living God speaks to the truth of transformation through experience. In response to seeing *"the Lord sitting upon a throne, high and lifted up"* and hearing the Seraphim calling to one another, *"Holy, holy, holy is the Lord of hosts; the whole earth is full of his glory,"* Isaiah's natural response was, *"Woe is me! For I am lost; for I am a man of unclean lips, and I dwell in the midst of a people of unclean lips; for my eyes have seen the King, the Lord of hosts!"* And upon declaring the truth of his depravity a seraphim touches his lips with a burning coal and says, *"Behold, this has touched your lips; your guilt is taken away, and your sin atoned for."* Isaiah was transformed through experiencing God.

If you want your life to be transformed you must set out to seek the face of God. You must respond daily to his invitation to meet together. Your life must be centered around the fact that perfect, blameless Jesus gave his life that you might simply have relationship with the Father. If you do—if you give your life to experience the fullness of God's love, power, and presence—you will never be the same. May you *"[behold] the glory of the Lord"* today as you enter into a time of guided prayer (2 Corinthians 3:18).

GUIDED PRAYER

1. Meditate on the transformation that takes place in experiencing God.

"And we all, with unveiled face, beholding the glory of the Lord, are being transformed into the same image from one degree of glory to another. For this comes from the Lord who is the Spirit." 2 Corinthians 3:18

"Behold, this has touched your lips; your guilt is taken away, and your sin atoned for." Isaiah 6:7

2. Turn your heart to God and seek his face. Have faith that when you set aside time to experience God he will manifest his presence to you. His presence is his promise.

"You have said, 'Seek my face.' My heart says to you, 'Your face, Lord, do I seek.'" Psalm 27:8

"You will seek me and find me, when you seek me with all your heart." Jeremiah 29:13

3. Rest in the presence of your loving Father. Confess any sin you have in response to his holiness and promise to forgive you. And receive the cleansing that comes from repentance.

"Repent, then, and turn to God, so that your sins may be wiped out, that times of refreshing may come from the Lord." Acts 3:19 (NIV)

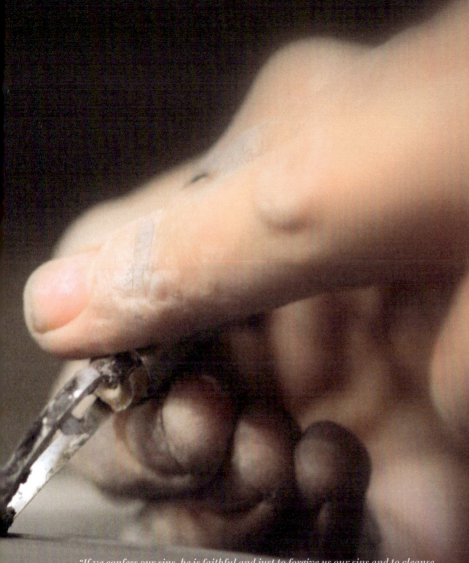

"If we confess our sins, he is faithful and just to forgive us our sins and to cleanse us from all unrighteousness." 1 John 1:9

So great is God's love for you that he longs to meet with you. In Revelation 3:20 God says, *"Behold, I stand at the door and knock. If anyone hears my voice and opens the door, I will come in to him and eat with him, and he with me."* God is already knocking on the door of your heart. You don't have to wonder if he will meet with you when you open your heart to him. Revelation 3:20 is his promise. He longs for you to encounter him more than you do. He wants to be known by you more than you want to know him. Have faith in the goodness of your God and live a lifestyle of encounter. May your life be transformed by a revelation of God's unfailing love and presence.

Extended Reading: Revelation 3

God Meets Us in Our Weakness

DAY 26

DEVOTIONAL

The ways of God are radically different than what we experience in the world. The world tells us that only the strong survive. The world values those who can take care of themselves. We're taught to look to our own strength as our source. We're taught never to let others see our weakness. But God values those

> *"My grace is sufficient for you, for my power is made perfect in weakness."*
>
> **2 CORINTHIANS 12:9**

who acknowledge their weakness in humility. His heart is for the destitute, the needy, and the lost. Jesus spent his valuable, limited time with the prostitutes, tax collectors, lepers, and sinners. And as a result, we who can never be perfect, who even at our best still can't cut it, have renewed hope.

In 2 Corinthians 12:9 Paul writes, *"But he said to me, 'My grace is sufficient for you, for my power is made perfect in weakness.' Therefore I will boast all the more gladly of my weaknesses, so that the power of Christ may rest upon me."* True growth and transformation aren't the result of working in our own strength. We can't change ourselves no matter how hard we try. Transformation is only possible when we declare the truth of our weakness, stop living in our own strength, and receive the power of a loving, present God. Transformation comes when we make room for the Holy Spirit to fill us, empower us, and set us free, not because we are deserving of his help, but because he loves us.

Psalm 103:14 says, *"For he knows our frame; he remembers that we are dust."* God doesn't expect perfection from us. He knows perfection is unattainable. And instead of perfection he asks for honesty. Instead of valuing our strength he values our humility. What he asks of us, all of us can give. All of us can boast of our weaknesses as Paul did. All of us can look at our lives and declare our need for God's grace. And in doing so we receive power from on high. In acknowledging that *"we are dust"* we gain the help of an Almighty, all-loving, ever-present God.

Stop trying to attain perfection in this life. Stop finding your value and identity in what you do. And look to God as your strength. Allow his love, power, and help to be your source. Live in light of the truth that his strength is both able and available to you. May you enter into a season of peace founded on the limitless grace and power of your heavenly Father.

GUIDED PRAYER

1. Meditate on God's heart to meet you in your weakness.

"But he said to me, 'My grace is sufficient for you, for my power is made perfect in weakness.' Therefore I will boast all the more gladly of my weaknesses, so that the power of Christ may rest upon me." 2 Corinthians 12:9

2. In what ways are you living in your own strength? Where do you need to stop striving and receive the grace and help of God?

"For he knows our frame; he remembers that we are dust." Psalm 103:14

3. Declare your weakness to God and receive the power of his presence. Ask him how he wants to help you. Make space in your heart for the Holy Spirit to strengthen you and empower you.

Proverbs 22:4 says, *"The reward for humility and fear of the Lord is riches and honor and life."* God has riches, honor, and life in store for you as you live in his strength. He longs to lead you to fullness of life if you will be willing to enthrone him as Lord over your heart. May you be founded on the grace and help of God and experience fullness of life today in the presence of your loving Father.

Extended Reading: Psalm 103

Life in Christ

DAY 27

DEVOTIONAL

Through the resurrection of Jesus, we have been given the opportunity to live life in a new way. Romans 6:4 says, *"We were buried therefore with him by baptism into death, in order that, just as Christ was raised from the dead by the glory of the Father, we too might walk in newness of life."* The power of the resurrection is not just over our deaths, but over our lives. God didn't just pay for our freedom for all of eternity, but for right now—for this very moment. He's calling you and me to live a resurrected lifestyle. He's ushering us into a resurrection culture.

Romans 8:9 says, *"You, however, are not in the flesh but in the Spirit, if in fact the Spirit of God dwells in you. Anyone who does not have the Spirit of Christ does not belong to him."* 2 Corinthians 5:16-17 even says, *"From now on, therefore, we regard no one according to the flesh. Even though we once regarded Christ according to the flesh, we regard him thus no longer. Therefore, if anyone is in Christ, he is a new creation. The old has passed away; behold, the new has come."* Your life is changed because of Jesus' death and resurrection. Because Christ rose from the dead, you have been raised from spiritual death.

"I am the resurrection and the life. Whoever believes in me, though he die, yet shall he live."

JOHN 11:25

Too often we are content to live our lives apart from the present reality of new life in Jesus. Too often we are satisfied living according to the flesh when we have been given a whole new way of living according the very Spirit of God who dwells within us as believers. Romans 8:1-2 says, *"There is therefore now no condemnation for those who are in Christ Jesus. For the law of the Spirit of life has set you free in Christ Jesus from the law of sin and death."* We have been freed from condemnation through the new law of the Spirit ratified by the death and resurrection of Christ. *"There is therefore now no condemnation."* Let that sink in for a minute. Through the grace of God, not by anything you could ever do, you have been freed from condemnation. The only one who could ever truly condemn you is now your heavenly Father. You are the child of the only Judge, and he has offered you continual and uncompromising pardon because of his love for you.

And past being pardoned from condemnation, Romans 8 tells us that we have now been crowned as co-heirs with Christ. Romans 8:16-17 says, *"The Spirit himself bears witness with our spirit that we are children of God, and if children, then heirs—heirs of God and fellow heirs with Christ."* Because of the life we have been given in the Spirit, we are *"fellow heirs with Christ."* I'm not sure we even fully understand all that means for us. So often we live as if we are forced into submission to the world. We live according to the principles of the flesh rather than life in the Spirit. You have been freed from slavery to sin. You have been freed from the condemnation of the world. Christ defeated the enemy at the cross, and through him you have obtained total and complete victory. You are now crowned with Christ and given his authority to see heaven come to earth through your life.

And most importantly, Romans 8 concludes by telling us of the incredible love available to us in our resurrection and victory with Christ. Romans 8:37-39 says, *"No, in all these things we are more than conquerors through him who loved us. For I am sure that neither death nor life, nor angels nor rulers, nor things present nor things to come, nor powers, nor height nor depth, nor anything else in all creation, will be able to separate us from the love of God in Christ Jesus our Lord."* There is nothing you or anyone else could do to separate you from the love of God. Through Christ's resurrection, you have been offered unchanging and unshakable love. Living life in the Spirit is living with the constant knowledge that you are and will forever be loved.

Spend time today allowing the word and presence of God to stir up your desire to live according to the Spirit rather than the flesh. We'll look tomorrow at how we can practically live this new life available to us, but for today simply allow God to reveal his unceasing love for you.

GUIDED PRAYER

1. Meditate on the life available to you in the Spirit. Allow your desire to walk in fullness of life to be stirred up by God's word.

"There is therefore now no condemnation for those who are in Christ Jesus. For the law of the Spirit of life has set you free in Christ Jesus from the law of sin and death." Romans 8:1-2

"The Spirit himself bears witness with our spirit that we are children of God, and if children, then heirs—heirs of God and fellow heirs with Christ." Romans 8:16-17

"No, in all these things we are more than conquerors through him who loved us. For I am sure that neither death nor life, nor angels nor rulers, nor things present nor things to come, nor powers, nor height nor depth, nor anything else in all creation, will be able to separate us from the love of God in Christ Jesus our Lord." Romans 8:37-39

2. Reflect on your own life. Where are you still living your life according to the flesh? Where do you feel condemned or unloved? Where do you feel conquered rather than a conqueror?

3. Ask the Lord to guide you into life in the Spirit today. Life your live with a renewed mind according to God's word.

As you go throughout your day, know that you have the choice to live your life differently. You are not bound by the way you've lived your life in the past. There is *"newness of life"* available to you every single day through the power of the Spirit working in you as a believer. Yield to the Spirit's leadership and live in light of the freedom purchased for you by the death of Jesus.

Extended Reading: Romans 8

Life in the Spirit

DAY 28

DEVOTIONAL

We devoted time yesterday to searching Scripture for understanding on life in the Spirit. We looked at Romans 6:4 which says, *"We were buried therefore with him by baptism into death, in order that, just as Christ was raised from the dead by the glory of the Father, we too might walk in newness of life."* And in Romans 8 we learned that God has offered us a life free from condemnation (Romans 8:1-2), crowned us with Christ as his co-heir (Romans 8:16-17) and made it so nothing could separate us from the depths of his love (Romans 8:37-39).

We've been given an incredible life in the Spirit through Christ. But so often we continue to live as if his death and resurrection didn't change our everyday occurrences. So often we live according to the flesh rather than our new life in the Spirit. So, building on the foundation of God's word, let's take time today to learn some practical ways we can better live the abundant life afforded to us through the resurrection of our Savior.

> *"We were buried therefore with him by baptism into death, in order that, just as Christ was raised from the dead by the glory of the Father, we too might walk in newness of life."*
>
> **ROMANS 6:4**

How can we better live our lives in the Spirit? How can we experience the *"newness of life"* Paul talks about in Romans 6? It all starts with growing in our friendship with the Spirit. The Bible tells us that the Spirit prays for us when we don't know what to pray (Romans 8:26), that he teaches us (John 14:26), helps us (John 14:16), and fills us (Ephesians 5:18). But the Holy Spirit never forces himself on us. He only fills and speaks when he is asked. Such is the depth of God's love for us that he waits patiently for us to open ourselves to him, beckoning us with his loving-kindness. So, we must make time every day to be filled with the Spirit anew and learn what it is to receive his help, teaching, presence, and prayer. It's only when we grow in our relationship with him in private that we will learn how to be led and used by him in public. Just as you couldn't pick out an unfamiliar voice from a crowd, you will have a hard time feeling the nudges of the Holy Spirit in this rushed and busy world without experiencing him in the secret place. Growing in friendship with the Spirit is vital and foundational to living with *"newness of life."*

Next, we have to live in obedience to God's word. God has blessed us with an incredibly practical book meant to guide us into an abundant, Spirit-filled life. To walk in obedience to the word is to live a life experiencing all that God has in store for you. So, spend time in the word of God opening your heart to the Spirit. Allow him to be your teacher. And commit yourself to live in obedience to what he shows you. In obedience to God's word you will discover how perfectly applicable and powerful Scripture is to your life.

Lastly, set aside time to simply receive the love of God. We live our lives in a society full of people and possessions that promise to satisfy us. We're surrounded by a world that isn't living out of personal experience with God and isn't a reflection of his truth. If we're going to live in the world but not be of it, as Romans 12:2 commands us, we must spend time experiencing the reality of God's love. We must allow his presence to be the lens through which we see the world around us. Victory over the enemy comes from encountering the reality of God's unfathomable grace and affection. Following the leadership of the Spirit moment to moment stems from encountering the reality of his nearness in the secret place. You have to spend time engaging in spiritual relationship to live a spiritual life.

Spend time today growing in your friendship with the Spirit, reading God's word, and receiving the love of your heavenly Father as you enter into guided prayer.

GUIDED PRAYER

1. Spend time receiving a fresh filling of the Spirit. Simply open your heart and wait for him. Ask him to make the reality of his presence known to you. Ask him to lead you into deeper friendship with him. The Spirit loves to talk to us, help us, and guide us because he loves us. You will never have a better friend than the Holy Spirit.

"Or do you not know that your body is a temple of the Holy Spirit within you, whom you have from God? You are not your own." 1 Corinthians 6:19

"But the Helper, the Holy Spirit, whom the Father will send in my name, he will teach you all things and bring to your remembrance all that I have said to you." John 14:26

"If you then, who are evil, know how to give good gifts to your children, how much more will the heavenly Father give the Holy Spirit to those who ask him!" Luke 11:13

2. Spend time engaging with God's word. Where does your heart need more life? Where do you feel like the world has taken over? Look up Scripture on whatever subject you need help with, and stand on God's word! Renew your mind and live in obedience today.

"All Scripture is breathed out by God and profitable for teaching, for reproof, for correction, and for training in righteousness, that the man of God may be complete, equipped for every good work." 2 Timothy 3:16-17

3. Receive the love that God has for you today. Similar to receiving a filling of the Holy Spirit, just spend time resting in the presence of God. Ask him to reveal his love to you. Ask him how he feels about you.

"I am the vine; you are the branches. Whoever abides in me and I in him, he it is that bears much fruit, for apart from me you can do nothing." John 15:5

"As the Father has loved me, so have I loved you. Abide in my love." John 15:9

I pray that you would be transformed as you align your life with the resurrection culture. May you see yourself as one saved, redeemed, empowered, and delivered. May you live in pursuit of the abundant life available to you. May the chains of this world fall off in light of God's powerful grace. And may your life be a reflection of the reality of Jesus' life, death, and resurrection.

Extended Reading: John 15